MW00985420

BECAUSE YOU PRAYED

Books by Ruthie Jacobsen

Because You Prayed
The Difference Is Prayer
A Passion for Prayer (coauthor)

To order, call **1-800-765-6955.**
Visit us at www.rhpa.org for information on other Review
and Herald products.

BECAUSE YOU PRAYED

Heartwarming stories about our listening God

RUTHIE JACOBSEN *with*
PENNY ESTES WHEELER

REVIEW AND HERALD® PUBLISHING ASSOCIATION
HAGERSTOWN, MD 21740

The author assumes full responsibility for the accuracy of all facts
and quotations as cited in this book.

This book was
Edited by Penny Estes Wheeler
Cover design by Edgerton • Bond Image Design
Cover photo by Corbis
Electronic make-up by Shirley M. Bolivar
Typeset: 11/15 Garamond

R&H Cataloging Service
Jacobsen, Ruthie
    Because you prayed: heartwarming stories about
our listening God, by Ruthie Jacobsen with Penny Estes
Wheeler.

        1. Prayer.   I. Wheeler, Penny Estes, 1943-   .   II. Title.

242

ISBN 0-8280-1431-0

DEDICATION

To the many adults, teenagers, youth pastors, and others who have diligently prayed—especially my husband Don, our children, grandchildren, and extended family.

and

To our friends Bill and Bonnie Colson, who have believed and cooperated in special ways with the Lord in making Prayer Ministries a reality.

ACKNOWLEDGMENTS

Thanks to all those who have generously contributed their stories, their struggles, and their inspiration. The insights they have gained from prayer and a God who hears and answers are an encouragement and reality that God is truly "the same yesterday, today, and forever."

Thanks to my sister, Rose Ludlow, and to all who pray daily, faithfully and diligently, for this ministry, offering unselfish prayers of intercession for others.

Thanks especially to my husband, Don, for his prayers, editorial skills, and his gift with words.

Thanks to Penny Wheeler, whose friendship, enthusiasm, and talents have made this work a joy.

Most of all, I acknowledge my dependence on God for His leading and blessing. His answers at every step have made this book possible.

CONTENTS

INTRODUCTION

Have you ever asked yourself the question, "When I should be, and want so much to be strong, why do I seem at that moment to be weak?"

The apostles found themselves in that place when the church was in its infancy, and they were "covered up" with day-to-day survival. They were in danger of missing the very priority of their calling—the Word of God and prayer! They wanted to be strong but were feeling weak. So they called "the congregation of disciples" and expressed their frustration. They knew they were neglecting the Word of God in order to serve tables. So others were put in charge of those serving roles, and the apostles were able to devote themselves to prayer and to the ministry of the word (Acts 6:2-4).

Isn't this where each child of God should be strongest—in the Word of God and in prayer? It is in the Word of God that we find Jesus. Every principle needed for our daily life is found in the Word of God. It may not be spelled out in practical detail, however, so we need to talk with and listen to our heavenly Father in prayer.

The disciples wanted to be careful that they didn't become so occupied with serving and their daily work that they neglected really knowing God through His Word and through prayer. They wanted communication with Him.

Throughout this book you'll find stories and experiences of dependence on God and the realization that He is ever faithful. His very character is demonstrated in His names. His names are ways of looking into His heart to see the graciousness, the sympathy, the compassion, the hope, the power. His names tell us that He longs to reach us with the message that He still cares and is willing and able to hear, to answer, and to save.

This book is offered with the prayer that God will use it mightily to show us that the place of prayer according to His will is still the place of power. He has given us a wonderful promise to remind us of the importance of prayer, and of staying in His Word:

"If you abide in Me, and My words abide in you, you will ask what you desire, and it shall be done for you" (John 15:7, NKJV).

Chapter 1

FRED'S MIRACLE

Fred Macey, age 17 and a senior at Andrews Academy in Berrien Springs, Michigan, was strong and athletic. On a brisk September morning he'd just returned from jogging when his sister Martha heard the door open and then a thud as Fred collapsed onto the floor. She ran and found his crumpled body by the front door. Fred was breathing but unconscious. He was rushed to the hospital, where physicians worked feverishly over him to diagnose the problem.

Fred, at 17, had had a stroke! Not just a minor problem, but a massive stroke, followed by other strokes, each one weakening him more than the last until he had to be placed on a respirator. Late that night technicians hooked him to the machine that would do his breathing for him.

Fred's carotid artery was occluded, blocking the blood supply to his brain. He couldn't breathe on his own, speak, see, or even think. As his physicians worked, the family prayed, and were soon joined by others from the community lifting the young man up to God in prayer.

For two long weeks there was no change, no improvement. Fred's body was there, but his life was gone. Finally the physicians came to Dorothy and Epifanio, Fred's parents, with the words they'd dreaded: "There's no sign of brain activity. We'll have to stop the life support." Clinically, Fred was dead.

The family had faced crises before, but none like this. From the time that Fred and his sister, Martha, and brother, John, were very small, their parents had taught them to pray. Every morning before school the family gathered for worship. Sometimes Martha chafed a little under the "rules" of her family. Many of her friends could run off to school without this daily ritual, and at times Martha wished she could too.

But now she was seeing the strength that came to her family as they prayed. She also discovered that friends, fellow students, and people they didn't even know had rallied to Fred's support. And not just in Berrien Springs, but all across the country as word of Fred's critical condition spread.

Before the ventilator was turned off, the Macey family met one last time in the little hospital chapel, again pleading with God to save their son and brother. Only the parents were allowed in the room as the tubes were removed. As the physician pulled out the endotracheal tube that had kept oxygen flowing into Fred's lungs, "Epi," Fred's father, couldn't stand still another second. With an impulse driven by a father's love, he pushed past the physicians and nurses working around his son's bed. Rushing to Fred's now lifeless body, he grabbed his son's shoulders and from his breaking heart cried out, "Fred, are you going to die? Please let God prove His power!"

Fred opened his eyes! In wonder, all watched as Fred began to breathe on his own for the first time in three weeks! The Great Physician was in that room that day.

Dorothy looked at her son and said, "Fred, what would you like?"

He smiled and answered, "I'd like water."

What rejoicing!

(I asked Epifanio not long ago what he wants most for his family and his response was quick and sure. "I would want my family to always believe in the Lord of the impossible.")

Fred still had a long road ahead. His recovery was slow. He had to overcome the results of massive strokes. He'd lost nearly all capacity to speak or to walk. So he began the long, hard road through rehabilitation. As this story is being written, his speech is slowly improving, and he has been able to return to school—this time to Berrien Springs High School, where specialists are better able to care for his special education needs.

Fred attended school faithfully and worked hard on recovery. Friends rallied around to cheer him on. When he'd meet people on the street, they'd give him the thumbs-up sign to let him know they were rooting for him.

Graduation approached, and Fred was determined to march with his classmates although walking was still very difficult. He would not be denied the thrill of receiving his diploma in person. So he practiced by the hour. He listened to "Pomp and Circumstance," insisting that his feet do what he told them to do.

At graduation the class decided to have Fred march last, to give him all the time he needed. The packed gymnasium was stirred as Fred, limping but triumphant, made his way down the long aisle, marching in perfect time.

When the principal announced his name, the audience, with pent-up emotion erupted in a standing ovation that lasted longer than anyone present could remember. The whole town seemed to be saying its collective thumbs-up to

Fred and his persistence, but also acknowledging a deep realization that the power of Fred's God is infinite.

At Andrews Academy a Fred Macey Day is observed every year to honor his recovery and to remember his miracle. His story has blessed the entire town of Berrien Springs and countless lives beyond. Others share their stories of praise on this special day, and they again worship the God who can do anything.

But the story doesn't end there. Fred's life is still touching others with hope. At a prayer and ministry conference for teens, Teens Pray '98, Martha talked to the high school and college students gathered at the conference, sharing the story of how God had touched their family and their town. As she concluded, Caesar, a student from Hawaii, invited to the front of the auditorium all those who wanted to turn their lives over to this God who has such love and power. Virtually everyone assembled there came forward, a tangible sign of their decision to let God be in complete control of their lives.

Gary Burns, a youth pastor and friend of Fred's, had an idea. He went to Apple Valley Market, where Fred worked bagging groceries. Gary told Fred the beautiful experience of that Friday afternoon and how God had used his story to lead many of his fellow teens to a new walk with God. Then Gary asked Fred a favor.

You see, even though Fred could speak very little, he could sing one song, his favorite—"Amazing Grace." Gary asked Fred if he'd come to that evening's meeting and sing that song. Knowing it would be an emotionally difficult experience, Fred thought a lot about it. For a stroke victim, emotions can be especially difficult to manage, but Fred knows that he is alive only because of God's amazing grace, so he agreed to try.

As Gary Burns introduced Fred later that evening to more than 900 teens meeting in the Pioneer Memorial church, there was reverent but enthusiastic applause.

Then Fred began to sing: " 'Amazing grace . . . how sweet the sound . . . that saved a wretch like me . . . I once was . . .' "

Overcome with emotion, he couldn't continue. There was only a hint of a pause in the music and every teen in the sanctuary picked up Fred's song: " 'I once was lost, but now am found; was blind, but now I see.' "

They finished the song, but God had done a work in their hearts they would never forget. None went away unmoved or untouched by the Master's hand and His amazing grace. In a sense they all participated in Fred's miracle.

Recently, as the Macey family shared this experience, Fred was asked once again to sing "Amazing Grace." At the conclusion of the song I asked him if he'd like to say something. He smiled as he slowly spoke three words: "One . . . more . . . chance."

God has given Fred one more chance to live, and he realizes that every day is a miracle.

God is still in the life-changing business. He still extends His amazing grace to each of us. He gives us whatever we need.

Elohim—He is the Creator and Lifegiver.

It's one of His names.

PROMISE

"Praise the Lord . . . he forgives all my sins . . . He ransoms me from death" (Psalm 103:1-22, NLT).

Chapter 2

KNEE TO KNEE

"Each time before I was sworn in as governor of the state of Missouri, we had a very special prayer service," says Senator John Ashcroft. "My father . . . , with all the enthusiasm and faith of his life as a pastor and president of a Christian college, was always there to add his blessing. It became a very significant time when God met us there as a church family. Our family would gather at the front of the church, and friends would gather around us and pray for God's special anointing, power, and protection.

"I knew what this had meant to me in the past," Senator Ashcroft explained when we visited together. "So when we came to Washington, D.C., and I was to be sworn in as a senator, I wanted that service again. We gathered—only about 12 of us—in a house on C Street. My father suggested that we sing before our prayer.

"I knew that meant that he would sing and I would play the piano for him, so I said, 'OK, Dad, what should we sing?'

"He said, 'Let's sing "Holy Ground," because Washington is a place of arrogance and God is calling you to a life here of humility and standing for what is right. If you are to live up to His call for you, you need His holy ground.'

"Then we formed a circle, kneeling for prayer. My 80-year-old father, frail now and weakened by a previous heart attack, was sitting in a low, large, soft chair. As I knelt in front of him, I could see his effort and struggle to get up. I said, 'Dad, you don't have to work so hard to stand.'

"He said, 'Son, I'm not struggling to stand, I'm struggling to kneel.' And we knelt together, knee to knee. And I thought that in this age when it seems so important to deal with one another, 'eye to eye' or 'toe to toe,' my father and I were together knee to knee, and I thanked God for my legacy, my rich inheritance.

"That was my father's last full day of life," Senator Ashcroft concluded. "He died on the way home from Washington, D.C., the next day, after I was sworn in as a senator from Missouri. I thank God for the lessons my father taught me—some by his words, and some by his life."

One of the things Senator Ashcroft remembers is his father's daily ritual. Every morning his dad did two things without fail. He prayed and he shined his shoes. The senator smiled as he explained to me, "I guess he wanted to be prepared spiritually and he wanted to put his best foot forward."

Senator Ashcroft, in his book *Lessons From a Father to His Son,* gives his memories as a 7-year-old. Let's let him tell it right from his book:

"So many years ago, as I eased out of the netherworld of a 7-year-old's sleep, I heard those earnest but discordant tones that signaled my father's morning ritual. His words, punctuated with passion, made their way up to the second floor, greeting me as I fought my way back into the world of consciousness.

"Dad's prayers were not the quiet, whispered entreaties of a timid Sunday school teacher. My father prayed as if his family's life and vitality were even then being debated on high as he bowed low.

"Hearing him pray was a magisterial wake-up call. While many kids wake up to the smell of coffee brewing or the sound of a rooster crowing, I have cherished memories of entering the day as this man's outspoken prayers filtered throughout the house.

"Sometimes I would ease downstairs and join him. One knee was usually raised, so I would slip in underneath him. In this way I was shielded by his body as he pleaded for my soul. Sitting so close to him provided a serenity and comfort and captivated my heart.

"If there was extra time, my dad would sing hymns of the church while accompanying himself on the piano. Mom made sure we never left for school without a fully satisfied stomach, but Dad was concerned with feeding our spirits, leaving a gospel tune embedded in our thoughts as we left the harbor so fondly known as home."

What an inheritance! No wonder Senator Ashcroft leads out in prayer breakfasts on Capitol Hill. No wonder he is willing to stand alone, if necessary, on a moral issue. No wonder he has a love for God and for gospel music. He leads a group called The Singing Senators that performs around Washington, D.C., and beyond. God is using him in the ministry of his music and in the political arena.

It was a privilege to meet him and to hear his story again. I had heard him speak at the National Day of Prayer event in Washington, and now I wanted to capture it on videotape so others could meet him and be blessed. He and his staff were gracious and delightful. The Hart Senate Office Building where he works is connected by a tunnel to all of the other senate offices and to the Capitol. At the bank of elevators in this building you see an elevator marked FOR SENATORS ONLY. And just to make certain you understand that, right under *that* bold sign is another that states: AT ALL TIMES.

But in the Honorable Senator John Ashcroft's suite of offices you find a "servant" mentality. The staff's goal is to serve, and it is obvious. The senator sets the tone. He creates the environment in which the needs of others are met, and even in the political arena God is at work.

As He did in the days of Daniel, God still uses His children in the high offices of government to make His influence felt. He is the same, "yesterday, and to day, and for ever" (Hebrews 13:8). He is faithful. He still hears and answers prayers.

Little Jessica and Jordan love to pray. Their parents have taught their children to love Jesus and to talk to Him as a friend.

Even before they were born, my niece Teri and her husband, Tedd, gave them to God. Prayer has been the center of their home and family. Teri learned this as a small child and wanted to pass it on to her children. So from the time they were babies, Jessica and Jordy were taught about Jesus. They love to ask the blessing at mealtime, and when Mom or Dad asks for a volunteer to pray at mealtimes, one or both clamor to do it.

Of course, as children do, they sometimes go on and on, thanking Jesus for everything imaginable—all that they've enjoyed that day, their family and friends, and every little thing they can think of. Jesus is important in their lives, and they love to talk to Him. I think He must smile as He hears their childish praise and requests. God has put such a sweetness into their hearts that they are irresistible, and seem to be infused with His love for others.

They live in North Dakota, where Tedd teaches at a Christian boarding academy and coaches the gymnastic team. The team of high school students take their performances and their anti-drug message to malls, schools, and other groups. Jessica and Jordan are part of the team, and they love it. Because physical exercise and activities are so important to their daddy, they both enjoy it too.

Teri is a pediatric occupational therapist, working part-time in nearby Bismarck, and on the days when both parents are working away from home the children are with friends or relatives for a few hours. But before leaving home each morning, the family always gathers in a circle, holding hands. They ask Jesus to protect them, and to lead them in everything they do.

A year or so ago when Jordan was 3 and Jessica 5, Teri enrolled them in swimming lessons at the local YMCA. They were thrilled. Jessica had done this the year before, so this was her chance to help her brother, and she loved that role. For Jordy this was a brand-new experience, and he was excited.

On the first day of swim lessons Teri dropped them off, then went to take care of some errands. When she stopped by at the end of their class to pick them up, she was met by their swimming instructor, who wore a big smile. The young woman was surrounded by children and was busy helping them into their coats—this was winter in North Dakota—and escorting them to waiting parents.

Suddenly she looked up. "I want to meet the mother of Jordan Webster," she said. Teri smiled and introduced herself, wondering what was coming next. She and the instructor chatted for a few minutes; then the instructor told this little story.

"I put the little plastic bubble on each child to keep them afloat. I explained that it would always keep them up, and they could move around in the water and have fun. I told them that the very first thing I wanted them to do was to kick and 'swim' all the way to the other end of the pool. When they got there, they were to form a little circle and hold hands.

"Well, they got down there faster than I expected and were all in place as I swam toward them. There was this little circle of happy children with their plastic bubbles, holding hands, exactly as they'd been instructed. And just as I came up I heard little Jordan say, 'I know; let's talk to Jesus.' So we did.

"I joined them, and we thanked Jesus for being with us and loving us, and asked Him to take care of us. It just seemed very natural. It wasn't that Jordan was afraid or anything," she told Teri. But she seemed curious about what was behind this comment from such a small child.

Teri explained that every morning the family held hands in a circle and prayed. The instructor was touched, and Teri was thankful that even at the age of 3, Jordy was developing the right kinds of habits.

No wonder Jesus Himself said that we need the simple, trusting faith of children, a faith that takes God at His word. A faith that gives strength and meaning to every day of our lives. A faith that trusts the God of our fathers who leads us.

How do you pass faith and dependence on God on from one generation to another? Or is it yours alone?

Judges 2:10 and 11 tells us that "after that generation died, another generation grew up who did not acknowledge the Lord or remember the mighty things He had done for Israel" (NLT). What a needless tragedy. God longs to care for His children, but He will not force Himself on them. God has special things in mind for us when we make prayer a priority, a special habit. When we wait at His feet to know Him, to listen for His voice in His Word, to get His instructions, His strength, and His help, we acknowledge our constant need of His guidance. He has promised to lead and care for us.

Even though one generation's devotion to God (or one family's devotion to God) does not make the next generation secure in Him, it *is* possible to leave a legacy of godliness. It is possible to leave consistent examples of dependence on God for guidance no matter where we live or what tasks fill our days.

In memory I still see my grandmother reading and rereading her German Bible. It was precious to her. My parents prayed daily, led the family in worship, and told stories of their friends who had inspired them, as new Christians, to pray.

Peter wrote that genuine faith will be rewarded by "praise, glory and honor when Jesus Christ is revealed," or when He comes (1 Peter 1:7, NIV). And yet the reward begins on this earth—in a life of joyful trust in God; in God-given peace that is beyond human understanding (Phil. 4:7). When we make prayer a priority, when we listen to His voice in His Word, no matter how busy or hectic our lives He will lead as He has led for generations. We gain strength from the examples of those who have gone before us to light the way.

> "God of our fathers, whose almighty hand
> Leads forth in beauty all the starry band
> Of shining worlds in splendor through the skies,
> Our grateful songs before Thy throne arise."

The second verse of this national hymn, written in 1876 by Daniel C. Roberts, speaks of His faithfulness in the past, and gives a plea for His help today:

> "Thy love divine hath led us in the past,
> In this free land by Thee our lot is cast;
> Be Thou our ruler, guardian, guide, and stay,
> Thy word our law, Thy paths our chosen way.

> "From war's alarms, from deadly pestilence,
> By Thy strong arm our ever sure defense;
> Thy true religion in our hearts increase,
> Thy bounteous goodness nourish us in peace.

> "Refresh Thy people on their toilsome way,
> Lead us from night to never-ending day;
> Fill all our lives with love and grace divine,
> And glory, laud, and praise be ever Thine."

He has led our fathers before us, and His plan extends to us today.

God of our fathers.

It's one of His names.

PROMISES

God's Spirit will pursue your children (Isa. 59:21).

God, as our loving parent, is willing to forgive.

Chapter 3

CORRIE AND I

How does a woman handle life as a new wife and very green stepmother of two teenage boys?

How does a family that's been fragmented by the death of a mother grow into a new whole?

How can this puzzle fit together: one excited, happy, slightly apprehensive bride; a joyful husband and father; and two still-troubled sons?

I didn't like to think about fairy-tale stepmothers. Everyone knows the Cinderella story all too well. It hadn't seemed so complicated when I began dating Don, a pastor whose wife had died after a car accident. Their boys, still trying to put their lives back together without their mom, were 13 and 16 when their father and I married.

I had prayed for a minister husband with teenagers. As long as I could remember, my dream was to be a pastor's wife. I'd admired these cheerful, caring women whom I remembered from my childhood, and had appreciated their ministry to the churches their husbands pastored. Their example was an inspiration to me—and an aspiration. I didn't realize all the responsibilities and privileges that came with it.

As a single woman, I'd worked with teens in the church youth department and loved it. I enjoyed their quick minds and the way they saw the world as packed with possibilities. Teens were energetic and willing to take on ministry projects—even helping at the rescue mission in the city of Dayton, Ohio. We always had a great time working together. So being a mother of teens, I reasoned, would be a piece of cake.

Wrong.

I discovered that there's a big difference between spending time at church and on projects of ministry with a whole group of teens, and taking 24-hour responsibility as a mother of two.

Being a parent of teenagers was more than a little scary.

I loved their father, and I loved *them*. And yes, Jerry and Randy were polite and fun to be with. They were trying to do their best, too. I thought this would be easy.

It wasn't.

Two wonderful boys—and they were! A wonderful husband—and he was! A brand-new, inexperienced wife and mother. That's an interesting combination.

With every passing day I discovered anew that without God's help I was helpless to be what this family needed. And I could see—in ways I'd never seen before—that I was *not* the loving and loveable Christian I wanted so much to be.

In my own steep learning curve I found myself with an exacting and impatient attitude. It may not have always been obvious to them, but I knew that my heart wasn't right. To make it worse, Jerry and Randy were still adjusting to the void their mother's death had left in their lives.

I had to adjust to a ready-made family; they had to adjust to a new mom.

The teen years are difficult enough for most kids, even if everything in their lives is stable. My boys were in that transition time, and their lives had been in upheaval. They still struggled with grief and loss.

Don was helpful. He listened to me. He spent time with the boys, playing ball, camping. He even took them with him on business trips whenever he could.

In addition, he loved to help in any way possible, and he was pretty creative. Jerry and Randy were cooperative and helpful with household chores. But inevitably tensions arose. I was introducing new ideas; this was *not* what they were used to. I probably did things their mother would not have done, or did things differently. I felt insecure in my new role and was afraid they needed more than I could give.

I wished so much for an older woman to mentor me. Someone who would listen without judgment, but point me in the right way. A friend who could help me see the right decisions to make. I thought of Paul's letter to Titus: "Older women must train the younger women to . . . love their husbands and their children" (Titus 2:4, TLB).

I needed a godly woman willing to disciple me. But where would I find just the right person, someone I could trust to give me sound, loving, and wise biblical counsel?

After all, I was the pastor's *wife!* We were at Columbia Union College by now, where Don and I were both teaching. I didn't know where to turn, but I wanted some help.

Naturally I went to God with my daily problems and concerns. My parents had taught us as children that He is the one who can help. Our relationship grew deeper—God's and mine—and I often felt His help. But I wanted someone I could talk with now and then, even if only by telephone.

I know now of the strength that comes from a prayer partner. Someone who will pray for and with you, and point you to Scripture. Someone to hold you accountable and love you unconditionally. Without realizing it, *that's* what I needed.

There come times in our lives when we need a "Barnabas," an encourager; someone sensitive to our needs. All of us have times when our strength falters. We may grow weary and discouraged. It helps to have someone who understands. It inspires us to have strength to go on. An encourager lifts us up. Encouragers stir us to renewed commitment and new resolve, and inspire us with new courage and hope. An encourager brings a beautiful gift—renewal through encouragement. And while God is our greatest encourager, sometimes it's good to have a person, too.

I prayed for guidance, for wisdom, for love—and held tightly to God's promises. During that time I was especially blessed by books I'd been reading by Corrie ten Boom. I rejoiced in the story of her faith during World War II. How despite her imprisonment and inhuman treatment at Ravensbrook, a Nazi concentration camp, for the crime of hiding Jews; despite the death of her father and her sister Betsie at the hands of the Nazis; her trust in God didn't waver. I thought how wonderful it would be to meet her, or simply to talk to her somehow.

Weeks passed. I continued to cling to God as I felt my way through instant parenthood. And I continued to be blessed by Corrie's beautiful books. They were Scripture-based, positive, and instructive.

Then an impossible thought whispered through my mind. I wished *I* could talk to Corrie. Could it be possible?

The more I struggled, the more convinced I became that she could help me. So taking my courage in hand, I called her publisher.

The Lord who sees our need must have inspired my thought, then opened doors. For somehow God impressed the person who answered the phone to take the time to get briefly acquainted with me. I explained who I was and that I would like to be able to contact the author of these encouraging books. She gave me the name of a woman in Pueblo, Colorado—a friend of Corrie's with whom she lived when in the United States.

It was simple enough to call directory assistance, and to my surprise, within seconds I had the number. (I couldn't believe it wasn't unlisted.) With a prayer in my heart I dialed it, talked to Corrie's friend, and learned when she would be in Colorado again. Amazing!

The next few weeks were an exciting time of waiting and anticipation. They were also more than a little scary, for questions filled my mind. What if Corrie felt that I, a complete stranger, was imposing on her time? (For surely I was, I reasoned.) What if she were deluged with people who wanted to get acquainted, to ask advice, or to visit with her? How could I ever establish a relationship with this busy woman, a celebrity, who knew nothing of me and my situation? Was I being presumptuous? Was it a childish dream to imagine that she could actually help?

But the God who sees had a plan. Only He could have orchestrated it, for He was way ahead of me with His beautiful answer to my prayer. He was in control. No wonder Paul could say, "What a wonderful God we have—he is the Father of our Lord Jesus Christ, the source of every mercy, and the one who so wonderfully comforts and strengthens us in our hardships and trials. And why does he do this? So that when others are troubled, needing our sympathy and encouragement, we can pass on to them this same help and comfort God has given us" (2 Cor. 1:3, 4, TLB).

The day finally came. Corrie would be in the States, staying with her friend. Would I have the courage to do it? My heart pounded a little faster. My hands trembled. But with a prayer on my lips I mustered my courage and dialed the number. When her friend answered, I gave my name and asked if it would be possible to speak to Corrie ten Boom. A little voice in my mind kept saying *What audacity!* But I clutched the receiver, not wanting to give up now.

Suddenly the sweet, familiar voice with the heavy European accent I'd heard on tapes and Christian radio was actually on the other end of the line. She listened attentively. She didn't seem rushed, and I felt that she just wanted me to be comfortable with her. I told her my little story, sharing my fears and concerns. She gave me godly advice. She even prayed for me.

I was thrilled. Not only with the sweet encouragement this godly woman gave me, but with the knowledge of our personal God who cared enough about me to meet me in my need.

We visited together by phone a few more times. She always seemed concerned and responsive to my call.

Our lives could not have been more different. I'd lived a sheltered, comfortable life. I was a nurse and teacher and now a mother, while Corrie was a Dutch clock maker. A spinster. An elderly woman who had survived the starvation and brutality of Nazi concentration camps. Could we have been more different? Perhaps not, but our conversations literally changed my life.

She had a simple, humble walk with her strong God that was real and full of power. Even on the telephone she created a climate of trust and implicit faith. "God is stronger than the darkest power," she wrote in *The Hiding Place.* She knew that He would never fail. She knew that He is the God who sees our need, and she helped me see my situation in a different light. She helped me deal with fear.

I wish I could say that I immediately learned to be the model Christian wife and mother. But I'm still learning. My boys, whom I love, are both happily married and have homes of their own. They still bring us great joy. I thank God for my children, their wonderful wives, and our two beautiful granddaughters. God is good.

He is our compassionate friend who sees us. He is aware of our needs and loves to meet the needs of His children.

El Roi, the Strong One who sees.

It's one of His names.

PROMISES

It is human to grow weary and discouraged. What a heaven-sent blessing is a friend who encourages and cheers.

"When they were discouraged, I smiled at them. My look of approval was precious to them" (Job 29:24, NLT).

"Praise be to the God and Father of our Lord Jesus Christ . . . who comforts us in all our troubles, so that we can comfort those in any trouble with the comfort we ourselves have received from God" (2 Cor.1:3, 4, NIV).

Chapter 4

GOD'S
GIFTED HANDS

I felt awestruck as I walked through the doors of the prestigious Johns Hopkins Medical Center. Here medical miracles are daily occurrences. Here some of the best minds in medicine battle with rare illnesses on a daily basis.

My appointment there was to make a video tape with Dr. Benjamin Carson. In 1987 Dr. Carson gained worldwide recognition for his part in the first separation of Siamese twins joined at the back of the head. It was an extremely complex and delicate operation—five months in the planning and 22 hours in the execution. His pioneering work in other areas of neurosurgery has made him known around the world.

But as Jessie Jackson wrote in his endorsement of *Gifted Hands,* "Of equal value [to his surgery skill] is the time he spends talking to kids, teaching them how to set goals . . . how to rise above bad family situations, and how to use their God-given abilities to be the very best they can be."

My first "meeting" with Dr. Carson had been through an audiotape of a lecture he'd given, and I was captivated. In a soft, unhurried manner he told of how God had changed his life and led him to the position he held today. I felt such power in his words and message that I wanted to meet him and his family in person. That opportunity came sometime later when we attended a birthday party for mutual friends. But it was a casual, social meeting. Nothing else. Now I had the appointment to interview him for a segment on prayer for the Adventist Communication Network. I was eager to talk with him about the place of God in his life.

Entering the spacious, awesome Johns Hopkins complex, I stopped at the information desk to get directions to Carson's office. The receptionist smiled. "Oh, yes. We all know Dr. Carson. He's my favorite person here. A kind, genuinely wonderful person."

As I took the elevator, then walked down the corridor to his office, I thought of his autobiography, *Gifted Hands*. He grew up in Detroit's inner city, failing in school until his mother limited his TV and required him to read library books every week. And he had a terrible temper. Anything could set him off.

He was 14 years old when the crisis came. A young friend, Bob, wouldn't change the station on his radio, and that made Ben mad. In a rage he grabbed the camping knife he always carried in his back pocket and with every ounce of muscle lunged at the boy. The knife glanced off the large buckle on Bob's belt. The blade snapped from the force of the blow and fell to the ground.

Dr. Carson writes that he stared at the broken blade and went weak. With startling clarity he realized that he'd tried to kill his friend. Without a word he turned and ran home.

He locked himself in the bathroom so that he would be alone, and wept. For two hours he wrestled with himself, with the rage that often controlled him and now threatened to destroy him. Since age 8 he'd dreamed of becoming a doctor. But he knew that unless he could control his temper, he would never fulfill his dream.

After two hours of misery and self-hatred, from somewhere deep in his mind came a strong impression: *Pray.* He hardly thought it was possible to change. He'd read enough of psychology to know that experts believed it was difficult, if not impossible, to modify personality traits.

"Tears streamed between my fingers," he writes. And he prayed. "Lord, despite what all the experts tell me, You can change me." The young Ben reminded God that He had promised that if we come to Him in faith, He would answer our prayers. This was a desperate situation. He was pleading for his very soul.

Ben slipped out of the bathroom and got a Bible. He brought it back into the small room and began to read in Proverbs. These words impressed him the most: "He who is slow to anger is better than the mighty, and he who rules his spirit than he who takes a city" (Prov. 16:32, RSV).

At last he stood up. Somehow he knew he was free. He had given his anger to God, and God had accepted it. Anger would never control him again.

That same day he determined to read the Bible every day, a habit he still practices.

Now, as I interviewed him in a conference room of the Johns Hopkins complex, I sensed a radiance, a power and strength beyond his own. His voice was soft but confident. "My faith in God has been intensely personal and is an important part of who I am," he told me.

As we were finishing our conversation for the video

camera I said, "Ben, in just a few minutes you are going to walk out of this room. You will go to the operating room, where you will perform surgery with your 'gifted hands.' You'll make life-and-death decisions and will need much more than manual skill. How does that make you feel?"

"I know that I have to depend upon God. I pray through every surgery."

Dr. Ben invites God to be in complete control in his life. He acknowledges, as God's children have done throughout the ages, that the power is His, and that He is faithful.

"You can depend on God," he'll tell you. "No matter what your needs may be. He will never leave you or forsake you [Heb. 13:5]."

Prayer. It brought peace and victory to a violent inner-city kid. It brings peace and strength to you and me today.

Jehovah Shalom, the Lord who is our peace.

It's one of His names.

PROMISES

"Be completely humble and gentle; be patient, bearing with one another in love" (Eph. 4:2, NIV).

"Prayer is not only something I need every day, but all throughout the day" (Dr. Ben Carson).

In our often violent world, to be gentle is especially precious.

Chapter 5

HE'S LOOKING
FOR YOU

A young woman picked up the phone and dialed her friend. But instead of her friend's voice she heard a whispered "Hello" on the other end of the line.

"Hi, Mikey, is your mommy home?" she asked her friend's 3-year-old.

"Yes," he quietly replied.

"May I speak to her, honey?" she asked.

"No," he whispered. "She's busy."

"Well, is your daddy home?"

"Yes."

"Could I speak to him?" She was getting curious now.

"No; he's busy," Mikey answered, still whispering.

"Is anyone else there?" she wanted to know.

"Yes," he said softly. "The fire department."

Her heart beat a little faster now as she envisioned all kinds of disasters at her friend's home.

"Mikey, is one of them close to the phone?" she asked.

"No," he whispered. "They're busy."

She was starting to feel a little desperate. "Is anyone else there?"

"Yes," he said in his quiet little voice. "The police are here too."

"Let me speak to one of them, Mikey," she demanded.

"No; they're busy." Still whispering.

"Now, let me get this straight. Your mommy is home. Your daddy is there, and the fire department and police are at your house. Is that right?"

"Uh-huh."

"But they're all busy?"

"Uh-huh."

"What are they doing?" she asked, almost hysterically.

"They're looking for me."

And we have a God who is looking for us. At the beginning of earth's time God left heaven and came here to look for His two lost children. Even though He knew where they were, He didn't call to them from afar. He came to the garden He had made for them, seeking them, wanting to talk to them face-to-face. It would be one of the last times God could do so with earth's children, for sin had entered the world and separated them from their heavenly Father. He wanted them to know that nothing could compromise His love for them.

It was important to Him to be with Adam and Eve then, and it is important for Him to be with us now. Imagine it! A God who comes seeking for us now. He knows where we are, and what we are doing and even thinking. And why. But He will do whatever it takes to get our attention and to help us look up to discover that His view of us is the same as it was that evening so many years ago in Eden. That evening when He went searching for His first children.

The message of His heart to us is personal too.

I have been looking for you.

You are special, so special, to Me.

I have a specific purpose for you.

That is what prayer is about, the opening of our hearts to God in the same way as we do with a close and trusted friend. But let's ask some hard questions, for questions are good. They help us evaluate and find answers.

First, *Why pray,* if God already knows all about us and our needs? Second, *What about faith?* Don't some people just naturally have more faith than others do? Third, *Is prayer always practical?* Can its outcome be measured?

Let's consider these questions, and even as you read the answers here, ask them of your own heart.

1. Why pray, if God already knows all about us and our needs?

God wants us to get to know Him. Prayer enables us to come into His presence, and in His presence we are changed. When we send our thoughts, our words, to God; when we reach toward God—whether we are kneeling by our bed, taking a walk, or driving our car— we are entering on holy ground. For when you pray, you come into the presence of God. And where God is, is holy ground.

Prayer frees God's hand to do more in our own lives and in the lives of those for whom we pray. Alvin Van der Griend has said, "God rules the world through the prayers of His people." Christ actually meant prayer to be the great power by which His church should do its work.

Prayer doesn't change God; it changes us. We don't pray to tell God what He already knows, we pray to venture into His presence so He can help us understand what He already sees.

2. What about faith? Don't some people just naturally have more than others?

Faith is built on experience. If over time we interact with a friend who is consistently trustworthy and fair, we grow to deeply trust him or her. Our faith in God is built on experience, on trying Him and finding Him faithful. On opening our hearts to Him and receiving the strength and insights that He will give.

After many trips to physicians, a young couple from Tulsa, Oklahoma, was told the heart wrenching news that their baby had cerebral palsy. There followed a roller coaster of emotional experiences as they began to understand the implications of the diagnosis. But at the same time they learned that God can bring positive things out of even an agonizing situation.

In telling their story, this young mother said, "We saw small miracles, and were continually reminded that God's hand was at work." Then she made this profound observation: "I believe that God wants much more for us than what a carefree existence can produce." Facing problems, searching for solutions, clinging to God for strength and comfort—this is when faith begins to grow and we gain a glimpse into the eternal perspectives of God.

3. Is prayer always practical? Can its outcome be measured?

Yes, prayer is a practical experience. It is often literally hands-on.

Max Lucado, the popular Christian author, recently wrote, "When we work, we work. But when we pray, *God works!*"

41

In the battle between good and evil God has chosen to be responsive to the prayers of His people. The record is clear. When God's people pray the sun is stopped in its tracks (Joshua 10), walls fall down (Joshua 6), sinners become saints (Acts 9), and enemies are put to flight (2 Kings 7). Today's answers to prayer are no less specific. Families are put back together, and worries are put under His banner of healing. How's that for measurable?

Granted, sometimes God works more subtly. Not all prayers are answered as we want or at the time we want. We may wish that God would grab a loved one and *make* them do what is right, but God never violates our freedom to choose. We want a prayer answered *now,* but God knows that in the long run that would be a mistake. His timing may seem slow to us, but He is always right on time.

God isn't like a candy machine—put two quarters in and candy drops out. Pray today, "candy" tomorrow—God doesn't work like that. But God is a friend. Your friend. And when you talk with Him, when you listen for His voice, you are changed. You are empowered and ennobled. You will grow in ways that you never thought possible. Also, God has infinite patience. He works with our limitations, yours and mine. And as time passes, we often know. *I asked for this, but God gave me that. And He was* right!

God is too great, too loving, to invite us to come and talk with Him, share our hearts and souls with Him, and then ignore us when we do. He does not ignore those who cry to Him for help (Ps. 9:12).

Intercession.

It's interesting to observe that many of the great preachers in Christian history, those who were instrumental in changing entire nations—Spurgeon, Finney, Moody—were blessed with intercessors. With friends who constantly lifted them before God's throne, pleading for the power of the Holy Spirit to bless their ministry. That raises the question of who had the more valuable part to play—the preachers, or the intercessors through whom God empowered the preachers.

4. And this raises a final question. Is God calling you, right now, to the role of intercessor in His end-time church?

The Bible shouts with examples of intercession, but perhaps the most striking are drawn from John 17. John 17 records Christ's conversation with His Father in the Garden of Gethsemane. This prayer is divided into three parts. First, Christ prayed for Himself (verses 1-5). Next is recorded His prayer for those closest to Him—His disciples (verses 6-19). And John 17:20-26 records Christ's plea for all believers.

Listen to Jesus' prayer for the 12 men closest to Him: "I pray for them. I am not praying for the world, but for those you have given me, for they are yours" (verse 9, NIV). "My prayer is not that you take them out of the world but that you protect them from the evil one" (verse 15, NIV).

He concludes with a prayer for all believers—through the end of time. It's interesting what He asks for, out of everything He might ask of God. Christ prays for unity, "that all of them may be one, Father, just as you are in me and I am in you. May they also be in us so that the world may believe that you have sent me" (verse 21, NIV).

Stop a moment and think about that.

If you'd like an enjoyable afternoon, open your Bible to Exodus 32:7-14, Esther 4:15-17, Job 42, and to the beginnings and endings of many of the letters to the early

Christian churches and some of their leaders. Read the Old Testament records of intercession (and there are many), then note how many times Paul tells the church members that he is praying for them and how many times he asks for prayer for himself. This is intercession—holding up a person before God, asking for God to act in his or her life.

Moses did it.

Jesus did it.

It's biblical, and it's powerful. God calls you and me to do it too.

God's Word is packed with promises that He hears the voices of His children and that He answers prayers.

He not only intercedes as our Advocate, He is also our Helper.

It's one of His names.

PROMISES

Prayer helps us understand what God already sees.

"That is why we can say without any doubt or fear, 'The Lord is my Helper'" (Heb. 13:6, TLB).

The act of praying draws us closer to God.

God's Word is packed with promises that God hears the voices of His children and that He answers prayers.

Chapter 6

PRAYER
AT THE SQUARE

Sunday evening. It had been a full weekend, packed with music, prayer, and friends. Scripture had come alive to the teens. Christ was more real than ever before, and they had discovered the utter joy of sharing their love of Jesus with others.

But now the leaders of the teen prayer and ministry conference had packed up and left for home. Student delegates from other academies had gone too. Students at Mount Vernon Academy* were in their dorm rooms, visiting, unwinding, and getting ready for the coming week. Math and history assignments were due tomorrow, and also their essays for English class. The prayer conference was over, and life would get back to normal.

Or would it?

Nathan French, a senior at Mount Vernon, couldn't shake the experience, and didn't want to. Many other students felt the same way. Something had happened in those 48 hours. Nathan had discovered the God of surprises, for the Holy Spirit had touched his life. It was almost too much to believe, but he'd seen the Spirit touch other students

45

too, turning their lives inside out. Nathan had an unsettling conviction that life on campus must not go back to the way it was. They dare not lose what they'd gained. Just how that would happen, he wasn't sure.

It *had* been a special weekend.

Most of the students hadn't known what to expect when a teen prayer and ministry conference was announced. Perhaps a week of spiritual emphasis telescoped into a weekend? They'd been through those before. Sometimes classes were shortened to accommodate an hour-long chapel. Some speakers were great. Entertaining. Inspirational. Others, well, perhaps it depended upon your own viewpoint.

A weekend of prayer emphasis? Mount Vernon Academy kids could handle that. Just so no one expects us to *do* anything! Just so it doesn't get too personal.

Well, it did. Instead of one main speaker, students from academies in the Columbia Union as well as from Andrews Academy and Andrews University led the program. They confided what God was doing in their own personal lives and on their campuses.

It became something real and magnetic for the large group of students meeting there. Teens told of habits that were controlling their lives. They confessed drug and alcohol use. They shared the heartache of estranged and broken families, of illness and sorrow. And then, of miracles of God's rescue and His leading in their lives. Of forgiveness, and answered prayer. God's presence lived among them, and students were transformed.

One group of academy students visiting from a sister school had agreed to come for the fun of it. They'd brought a stash of liquor with them, expecting to find some new friends to party with. But on Friday night after the prayer and sharing time, something unexpected happened. The Holy Spirit touched their hearts. They sobbed out their story to their young youth pastor, Tom Decker. "We want to change," they told him. "We want the same thing that's going on with the guys we met tonight."

But back to Nathan. He'd been especially excited about the ministry experience on Sabbath afternoon. Hundreds of teens had fanned out in groups to "prayer walk" through Worthington, Mount Vernon, and Columbus, Ohio. Slowly walking down street after street, they had prayed for the families living there, for the people working in the businesses. They had claimed the streets, the people, for God.

If they walked past schools, they prayed for the faculty and students. They prayed for the gangs that sometimes controlled the kids, for God to fight the violence and protect students from drug use. They walked near taverns and nightclubs, and prayed for the men and women who were being destroyed by alcohol. With every step they fitted their prayers to the environment. For many of the students it was an afternoon that defied description.

Later that evening, as the prayer conference drew to a close, their stories bubbled out, the words tumbling over one another in an effort to help listeners experience it too. Hours passed. Up to 500 students had been involved, and many lined up for the opportunity to tell their story.

For many of these young people it was as though they had been on a train going one direction. Abruptly the train screeched to a stop. Jumping off, they leaped on a train coming the opposite way. Utter joy in the Lord, and hope for their futures shone from their faces.

It was late Saturday night when one of the teens stood up and read Luke 11:9, 10. "'So I say to you: Ask and it will be given to you; seek and you will find; knock and the door will be opened to you. For everyone who asks receives; he who seeks finds; and to him who knocks, the door will be opened' [NIV]."

Then he called the entire group of students to one large family prayer time. Through songs and spoken word the students thanked God for entering their lives in such a remarkable way. One by one they committed their lives to Christ. They prayed for their parents, their schools, their churches. They asked God for His special help as they reentered the world of classrooms and peers, of family problems and financial problems. In short, back to living in the nitty gritty world.

Monday morning. The spiritual beauty of the weekend stayed with Nathan, but the town of Mount Vernon lay heavy on his heart. The questions haunted him. *We're an Adventist Christian school in the heart of a city. People are dying who don't know God. What impact do we have on their lives beyond ordering french fries from their drive-ins and putting their gas in our cars? Is there truly anything we can do to make a difference?*

Nathan began to pray for Mount Vernon, for the people in the shops and the teens he saw on the streets. He talked to some friends and to his Bible teacher, Scott Christen. Nathan, Scott, and two friends—Isaac White and Carson Combs—went to the town square that first Sabbath to pray and to brainstorm, and God met them there.

They asked God to send a revival to their campus. Soon a speaker would be coming on campus, and they prayed for the Holy Spirit to speak through him; they prayed for his impact on the campus and community. The four prayed for wisdom to know the next steps to take. And they experienced the truth that whenever we turn our hearts to God in prayer He brings us up to Him. And wherever God is, is holy ground. They felt God's presence with them in the town square of Mount Vernon, Ohio. It was a joyful experience as they talked about what they might do next. Then Carson laughingly said, "Let's have prayer at the square."

Prayer at the square. It had a good ring to it. That was the beginning.

Nathan and his friends organized a retreat so that interested teens could come together for prayer and planning on how to minister to Mount Vernon. They divided into teams to study the Bible and pray together.

"God, Your Word says that Your promises are true, and James 1:5 tells us that if we ask, You will give us wisdom. We really need to know Your will in this situation, so we're looking to You to supply it. We thank You because we believe that You know exactly what we need. And You have promised to supply our every need. Teach us. What can we do to help the people of Mount Vernon know You better?"

They prayed, and they listened. And God led.

Experienced people coached the students on where to go and how to meet and talk with people. Every Sabbath afternoon at 3:00 this group met at the town square. They prayed together, then went door-to-door, up and down the streets of Mount Vernon. Introducing themselves, they said, "We're going to be praying in the square and have stopped by to see if you'd like to join us. If not, do you have a prayer request you'd like for us to pray for?"

People were disarmed by the thought of teens whose only reason for stopping by was to ask if they could specifically pray for them. For the people of Mount Vernon. Most were receptive. Many asked for specific prayer. Some joined the group to pray.

Were people surprised? Of course. Did they respond? Yes. And as the weeks went by, more and more people asked for prayer or joined the students in the square to pray with them.

"There were several reasons we did this," Nathan said. "First, we wanted to do something for our community. And we wanted to personally grow by reaching out to others. And we wanted to show the city of Mount Vernon that there are teens who care about them. We prayed for revival, and that God would meet the needs we gave to Him.

Other Christians joined them, men and women and kids who appreciated what they were doing and wanted to be with them to support what God was doing in their city.

Leaders on the academy campus were delighted to see what was happening. They asked Nathan if he'd like a new job. He'd been working at the cement factory, but he was offered the position of student chaplain. In his position he could give more of his time and energy to plan events for the Mount Vernon Academy campus and for other students as well.

They prayed for revival. They prayed for God to use them. And He did—in ways they could never have dreamed possible. They had their own prayer and ministry conference on their campus the next year—and with stirring results. For God had spoken to their hearts. He was leading, and they had followed.

The Shepherd had called, and they answered.
Shepherd.
It's one of His names.

---

*Mount Vernon, Ohio

PROMISE

"And whatever you do, whether in word or deed, do it all in the name of the Lord Jesus" (Col. 3:17, NIV).

Chapter 7

WHEN
GOD WHISPERS

As Candace came to the end of her quiet time that Sabbath morning she made a conscious effort to slow down her thoughts so she could hear God's voice. "Tell me, who should I pray for?" she asked God. "Who needs prayer this morning?"

At once her friend Dee came to mind. She didn't know what Dee had planned for that day or why she needed prayer, but immediately she upheld her friend to God. As secretary of her 400-member church, Dee carried a lot of responsibility. It had been especially busy and hectic in the months since their pastor had been assigned to another church.

When she got up from her knees Candace had a strong impression to call Dee and tell her what she'd done. It was only 8:00 a.m., but no one answered the phone. It took only a moment to leave a message. "Dee, I know you're carrying heavy responsibilities right now," Candace said, "and when I asked God to tell me who I should pray for this morning, your name popped right into my mind. I just had to call to tell you that I prayed for God to hold you in His everlasting arms today. I hope you have a happy Sabbath. You're very dear to me."

Candace was surprised to see Dee on the platform when she walked into Sabbath school. Dee sat with her during church, and Candace whispered to her that she'd prayed for her that morning. Dee looked at her in amazement. "I was so burdened when I woke up," she whispered to her friend. "I had a lot of things on my mind, and I needed prayer for all of them. I was waiting for Sabbath school to start when suddenly this peace came over me. It was so strange. Out of nowhere I had perfect peace."

They just looked at each other, awed by the evidence that God had literally touched them both that day.

Dee didn't pick up the phone message until sometime later, and was touched all over again. It was overwhelming to realize that God loved her so much that He cared for the small details of her life. The peace she'd experienced that morning had stayed with her all day long. She'd felt encircled in a calming love.

And it happened because Candace turned her heart toward God and asked Him to impress her with someone who needed prayer.

Many miles away . . .

It had been a long nine months since her mother died, and Trish still felt weary and heavy with loss. The death had been fairly sudden—after a brief illness. She'd gone to sleep on a Sabbath afternoon.

Leaving the hospital, Trish and her family had gone back to the house. It had always seemed so crowded when she and the three children came for a visit, but now it seemed cavernous. Empty. Their mother—wife, grandmother, sister—was gone, and every day for the rest of their lives they would live with the loss.

The telephone rang that afternoon, and a college friend asked for Trish. Mary was a nurse and had spent several years in overseas mission work. Home for a short visit, she'd heard that Trish's mother was ill, and called to express her concern

"She just died, Mary," Trish said. "She just died and—"

"I'm coming to see you," Mary said. "I'm about an hour away, but I'll be there as soon as I can."

Her visit and her sympathy had touched Trish's heart. She hadn't stayed long, just long enough to show that she cared. They'd written a couple times now that Mary was back overseas, but Trish found it hard to write. Her world was small. Housework. Children. There was little to write about.

For days Mary had lain like a heavy weight on Trish's heart. It was strange. No matter what she was doing, Mary's name dogged her mind. And it wasn't a good feeling. Mary—always upbeat and fun—was a burden on her mind that wouldn't go away.

She told her husband about it. "Why don't you write to her?" he asked.

"There's nothing to tell her."

"Well, then . . ."

But the burden persisted. She mentioned it to Jason again. "So write to her," he said.

Trish felt impatient. "I don't have a thing in the world to tell her. All I know is kids and school and cleaning and cooking. There's nothing to say that she could possibly be interested in."

"Well, then . . ."

The next day Trish sat down and banged out a long letter to her old friend. She truly had little to tell her, so she described the children and what they'd been up to. She told about making snow people during a heavy snowfall, and planting flowers and vegetables now that it was spring. *Just a lot of foolishness,* she thought to herself as she put it in an envelope and stuck on the overseas postage. *But at least it's done!*

Once the letter was mailed Trish didn't think of Mary again. It had felt good to write, but she wasn't sure what the whole thing had been about. Nevertheless, it was done and forgotten among all the chores of taking care of her family.

Four weeks later Trish received a letter from Mary. She opened it happily, wondering what exciting thing she'd been doing now. But what she read stunned her.

Mary wrote that she'd been in the depths of a depression unlike anything she'd ever experienced. Extreme exertion had brought on an illness, and after the illness, depression that she couldn't shake.

"But your letter turned me around," she wrote. "It was so *good* to hear about your family and the little things you are doing. It was exactly what I needed. Thank you so much for writing. I can't tell you how much it meant to me."

Trish sank down on the couch. What if she hadn't written? She hadn't wanted to write. She'd thought it was silly. She'd never even considered that God had placed Mary on her heart so that she could help her friend.

Trish pondered this over the next few weeks. It was almost beyond imagination that God had looked down upon two friends who lived many thousands of miles apart. God had seen that Mary needed help that Trish could give, and that Trish needed to know and feel God's touch in her life. To know without a doubt that even though she had lost her mother for a time, God's presence was there in her home with her, and would never leave.

He'd placed Mary on her heart.

He'd helped her write the letter, and think of funny, interesting things to tell.

Mary had been praying for help, not knowing where it might come from. And God urged Trish to be her answer to prayer. Impossible? Not if you believe.

Improbable? Not at all. Not if you know God.

For God's presence can be with you, as a sweet fragrance in your life. As the gentle scent of flowers is the sweet presence of God with us. He uses us in simple ways, as a fragrance in the lives of others.

The Lily of the Valley. Beautiful. Fragrant in your life.

It's one of His names.

PROMISES

"I have prayed for you" (Luke 22:32, NIV).

"I thank my God every time I remember you. In all my prayers for all of you, I always pray with joy" (Phil. 1:3, 4, NIV).

Chapter 8

DIVINE
TRAVEL AGENT

I'm sorry, sir," the owner said. "The horses always come in at night for food. I can't explain why they aren't here." He spread his hands in a gesture of helplessness. "This is very unusual; I don't know what to say."

Roger Wilcox, veteran missionary, administrator, and man of God, has been president of a Seventh-day Adventist conference, union, or division for more than 35 years. While he has served in the Middle East and Europe, most of those years have been in South America, including 10 years in Brazil.

It was while he was working in Bacabao, Brazil, that the experience told here happened. A fledgling Christian work had begun in Jeju, a village in the interior. It was a primitive village and the country was untamed. A church school had been established and an Adventist family, Jorge, his wife, and 2 children, had moved there to minister to the village. It was not an easy place to live and the progress of the gospel was painfully slow. Periodically, Roger and some of his staff made a trip to the interior, always going to Jeju to bring encouragement to Jorge and his family. Slowly the village people began to change as they fell in love with Jorge's God.

Travel plans to Jeju were always the same. First, prayer for safety in travel, prayer for wisdom in the numerous decisions necessary every step of the trip, and prayer that God would continue to uphold and encourage the missionary family living in isolation among people who knew so little of the gospel story.

On this particular trip, Roger and three colleagues traveled up the river by launch as far as they could go. There they stopped at a small village to spend the night, intending the next morning to rent horses and travel the last grueling miles into the interior. They found their hotel, then checked with the man whose horses they would rent. He assured them that the horses were let out to roam during the day, but that they would return in the evening for food and water. When the group came back in the morning, the horses would be saddled and ready.

However, when Roger and his companions arrived at the corral the next morning they were disappointed to discover that the horses had not returned the night before.

The owner could do little but apologize. "I'm sorry, sir," he repeated, helplessly.

What a disappointment! What to do? They walked back to the hotel and gathered in Roger's room to pray. What else could they do? To whom could they turn for help? They'd been especially concerned that the missionary in Jeju needed encouragement. It was important that they learn if he needed anything they could provide, and that they be able to worship and pray together. "Please, Lord, open a way to reach our friend Jorge, ministering in Jeju," was their earnest appeal.

After praying, they headed back toward the corral to see if the horses had returned. Rounding a corner in the small village, they came face-to-face with Jorge! What a reunion, as it began to dawn on them how God had providentially intervened. If they had picked up the horses as usual they would have completely missed seeing Jorge, for he was already in the village.

Our God is all-knowing, all-powerful—and a good travel agent. Not only does He uphold worlds by His power, but He cares enough for His children even to work out the little details.

Roger's next assignment was in Fortaleza, Ceara, near the Amazon River. As president of the North Coast Mission, it was his responsibility to oversee the work of the Adventist Church in that area, training pastors and church members to spread the gospel.

Though opposition was heavy, the little company of believers grew. Soon it was evident that they needed a church in which to worship, so they began looking for land. "I walked the streets for seven years," Roger says, "looking for land that would be suitable for a church, a school, and an office building for the mission. Time and again he found just the place. True, some pieces of property were better than others, but each time, when the seller discovered that it was for a church, the land would become unavailable. Roger and the others kept praying, reminding God of their needs and giving Him what seemed a totally impossible situation. Our God is not embarrassed by that kind of request.

After seven years of searching Roger discovered a large, beautiful piece of land in a prominent part of the city. It was not far from the governor's home—a perfect place for a church, a school, and an office complex. Encouraged, he set out to find the owner, and discovered that the man also owned a large lumber company.

Now it was time to redouble their prayers. The property was perfect. They desperately needed the facilities. How they prayed for God to open the way for them to buy this land.

Eventually the group met the owner in his office. He greeted them cordially and agreed to sell. The price he asked was 35,000 cruzeiros. They left the office praising the Lord! What a miracle! A beautiful piece of land adequate for their needs, in a lovely and prominent location. And the price was fair. They could do it.

Roger and his associates enthusiastically began raising the money needed to buy the land. *Praise the Lord!*

But not long after the conversation with the owner, Roger received a phone call from him. "Mr. Wilcox, I know I told you could buy that land for only 35,000 cruzeiros, but I need to tell you that there are some men in my office right now offering me 70,000 cash."

What a shock. What a blow. Roger hardly knew how to reply. After a brief conversation, both men hung up—and the prayers began anew.

As with all of God's stories, this one has a happy ending. The mission did indeed purchase the land at the original agreed price! Let me tell you why.

"I never could have sold that property to anyone but you," the owner told the mission leaders. "I'd given you my word. It's still yours for 35,000. Would you like to know why I refused their offer of twice the money?"

They would.

"Many years ago your church had floating clinics on the Amazon, and as the boats traveled up and down the river, they'd watch for villagers to wave a white cloth. This was the signal that someone in the village was ill, so the launch would pull over and stop. They'd stay as long as necessary, treating the sick and caring for their needs.

"On one such visit a boat, piloted by Dr. Halliwell, stopped to discover a seriously ill woman. She was actually near death. Dr. and Mrs. Halliwell stopped and took care of her for several days. They didn't leave her; they cared for her and prayed for her—and for the rest of her family.

"Miraculously, she recovered. That woman was my mother. And when I learned that Seventh-day Adventists needed a place to build a church I remembered the kindness and love, and the prayers they sent to a God who answers. That's why I could sell to no one else."

A beautiful church, which still stands, was built on the site. It became a center for ministry and evangelism in the area, and later the school and offices were added.

Roger says, "For seven years I prayed and the church prayed. We were never discouraged. We never felt desperate. We just kept praying and doing all we could to find property.

"It's a magnificent experience to see how an impossible situation removes the human element and God gets all the credit."

Anne would be the first to admit it. She wasn't a very brave person. So when her husband was transferred from Tennessee to Washington, D.C., she was nervous about staying by herself (with four children) in their house in the wooded hills north of Nashville. Now she knew God had more angels than there were trees in their woods, and that the angels would protect them. But she still wasn't comfortable.

She didn't mention it to anyone, but she did talk to God about it as she swept and dusted around the house. "What I really need," she told God, "is a dog. A nice, gentle dog that will stay inside with the kids and me at night. But of course there's no way because we're moving in a couple months. And who ever heard of a temporary dog?"

She went on with her cleaning, dusting the bookcases and knickknacks. "What I'd really like," she said aloud, "is a collie. They're so gentle."

As the days went by she continued to discuss her would-be dog with God. It was more like a talk between friends than formal prayer. She didn't even think of it as praying; more as thinking aloud.

The days passed faster than the gold-and-orange leaves could flutter down from the tall trees surrounding the house. Then a couple mornings before her husband had to leave for Washington, Anne opened the back door and saw a dog. A collie. It thumped its tail on the concrete stoop and looked up at her with soft brown eyes.

You'd have thought Anne would have yelled, "Yippee!" but her only thought was *We're moving! We can't have a dog.*

"Don't feed her," she told the children. "She's wearing a flea collar, so I know she has a home. Just leave her alone, and she'll go back where she belongs."

But she didn't.

Quietly, patiently, even politely, the big collie waited beside their back door. She never barked or demanded attention in any way and of course never tried to come in. Ten-year-old Noelle sat on the ground with the dog's head in her lap, calling her "my dog."

Little Jamie flung his arms around her neck, and Anne even sneaked a pat now and then. "Better go home, pretty girl. Someone's missing you," she told her.

After three days of that kind of nonsense Anne brought a few scraps of leftovers out for the collie to eat. She ate daintily, without hurrying, then sat back down beside the door. That was the beginning.

Finally Anne opened the door and invited her in. She paused, looking up with questioning eyes. "It's OK. You can come in," Anne invited. So the dog did. After sniffing around the house, she made herself at home. She slept beside Anne's bed or in the children's rooms. It was good to hear her soft, wheezy breathing at night. And Anne felt protected during the day for every so often Gretel (that name seemed to fit her) would bolt to a window, barking fiercely.

"What's out there?" someone would ask.

"Oh, Gretel's just scaring off another killer squirrel."

Gretel was a good watchdog. One day when a pickup truck came growling up the driveway Gretel raced to the door. Anne opened the screen and let her out, hardly believing how ferocious she sounded. She was always so gentle with them.

"Does she bite?" the driver asked, half in and half out of his truck.

"She hasn't yet," Anne replied.

They could tell that Gretel was getting old. Her legs were

stiff after a nap, and she'd get up slowly, moving carefully like an elderly lady. Her lower teeth were worn down to the gums. So Anne fixed her soft food to go with her doggie dinners. They all felt protective of "their" dog and began to try to figure out a way to take her along when they moved.

A few days before they were scheduled to leave, Gretel was playing in a ravine with the kids. She almost seemed to be laughing, running up the slope and racing back and forth on its rim. She barked at the squirrels chattering above her in the trees, and at dancing shadows and imaginary foes. Then Anne heard someone calling, "Here, Lassie. Here, Lassie. Come on, girl!"

Looking out the window, Anne saw a teenage girl holding a poodle and calling the collie. Gretel had come toward her, but stood, undecided, her mind still on the fun in the ravine. Anne went to the door. "Is that your dog?" she asked.

"Yes, and we've been wondering where she was," the girl said. "She comes home every few days for a meal, and then she's gone again."

"Well, she's been with us," Anne said. "She sleeps in the house, and we've even given her a bath."

They talked a few minutes. The girl lived in the house on the other side of the woods behind them and had followed her poodle down the trail to Anne's home. Lassie (alias Gretel) had been their dog for nine years, the girl said, but her "owner" had gone off to college. Anne could keep her until they moved, because the dog seemed so happy.

Someone has said that a coincidence is when God works out something really good for you but chooses to remain anonymous. You have to have your eyes open to recognize it. Knowing that God has answered your prayer with a big Yes makes you feel extra-special. Now and then God gives you these very personal answers to "little" prayers as an extra assurance that He is guiding your life.

A "temporary" dog.

Keeping horses from returning to their stable.

The God of the universe involved in such small details of our lives? Oh, yes. How valuable He is in our lives. Not only for these seemingly small things that mean so very much, but for the big things. Life itself. Courage and strength. Forgiveness. Salvation.

He is, to you and me, the Fairest of Ten Thousand.

It's one of His names.

PROMISES

"If you, then, . . . know how to give good gifts to your children, how much more will your Father in heaven give good gifts to those who ask him!" (Matt. 7:11, NIV).

A "coincidence" is what happens when God doesn't let you know He did it.

Chapter 9

THE LORD
FIXED THE FORD

In 1959, with about $300 in their pockets, Leo Ranzolin, his wife, Lucila, and their 2-year-old son packed up their belongings for a move from La Sierra, California, to Takoma Park, Maryland. Leo was going to study at Potomac University, formerly the site of the Seventh-day Adventist seminary.

They were traveling light. The few things they'd accumulated fit into their '51 Ford, and they were ready to go. That is, they were as ready as they'd ever be. Leo was a little nervous about the car, for it had given them problems before. On especially hot days it would "vapor lock" and refuse to run. So there they were, getting ready to cross the desert in the month of June in a car that locked up when it got hot.

Leo and his wife decided they might have less trouble and be more comfortable if they crossed the desert at night. (Most cars didn't have air conditioning.) The travel went well the first night, and they stayed in Salome, Arizona, the next day. They'd finish the trek across Arizona the next night, and could hopefully travel by day—and without problem—the rest of the way.

As soon as the sun went down, Leo started the car and

headed out. However, when he looked at the temperature gauge he saw that the engine was warming up. He knew what would happen next. Another vapor lock and a dead stop in the middle of the highway. So thinking that he'd beat the car to it, Leo pulled over, stopped, and turned off the engine.

Lucila was even more apprehensive than he was. She looked at the deepening darkness and at their young son and said, "Honey, let's go back to La Sierra and get another car."

Leo didn't reply at first; he just sat, pondering the situation. At last he spoke. "I can't afford another car, and if we go back we'll lose several days' time. That would make it difficult for me to start my master's at the seminary this summer."

But that wasn't the end of it, for he had another suggestion. "Let's pray. I know that the Lord will take us across."

Prayer had been a vital part of his life during the six years he'd sold Christian books in Brazil. Book sales had enabled him to get his education, and Leo knew God could help him again. So right there, inside the old '51 Ford, he, Lucila, and Leo, Jr., bowed their heads in fervent prayer.

"Lord, You know our situation. I do not have another car, and I don't have the time to go back," Leo prayed. I need to get to the seminary and prepare myself to serve You better. Please take over and help us get to Takoma Park."

They asked God to give their old Ford the power to make it across the desert *and* all across the United States. As soon as they said "Amen," Leo told his wife, "Honey, let's go." He started the engine, and away they went.

The needle in the temperature gauge remained at normal throughout the trip. "There was no problem whatsoever with our *old* Ford," Leo will tell you. "It had been fixed by the Lord. I know that it was only through the power of prayer that we crossed the country, going up and down mountains, on long stretches of plains, through cities and past farmland. It was with profoundly grateful hearts that we reached our destination.

They were aware of a loving God who was traveling with them, who knew just what was needed, and could help. Our God understands, and He is still with His people every moment.

Emanuel, God with us.

It's one of His names.

PROMISES

God wants to be with you (Lev. 26:12).

God offers His friendship to the godly (Nahum 1:7).

Wherever we go, God is there (Joshua 1:9).

Chapter 10

ONE
WOMAN'S DREAM

Vonette Bright had a dream. It was a magnificent dream, for its foundation had pillars in the very beginning of the United States of America. But more than a dream, it was a burden she could not put down. Vonette felt as if the Lord were shaking her by the shoulder saying, "The country needs an annual day of prayer, and you can help make it happen."

She couldn't say no to God.

The dream grew to a goal. It *could* happen. It *would* happen. Vonette felt in her heart that God had called her to push and urge, to speak softly and to shout when necessary, to bring about a national day of prayer.

Vonette and her husband were both Oklahoma kids. Their roots go deep in the heartland, with just enough Oklahoma brass to make them risk-takers for the Lord. Why else would they have had the nerve to start a ministry for Christians on secular campuses?

Ministries come and go, they were told, and theirs wouldn't last either.

That was in the 1950s, and Vonette and Bill Bright held tightly to their dream. Keeping their eyes on God and their feet firmly planted on the ground, they prayed and worked their way through obstacle after obstacle. Today, Campus Crusade for Christ ministers in 152 countries.

Vonette began her work in prayer ministry with a burden and concern and a *call.* Have no doubt about it, the call was there. And once she committed to it, there could be no turning back.

The nation was in chaos. The turbulent sixties had just ended. The Vietnam war—that confusing war in which children killed soldiers and soldiers killed civilians—was ending. American heroes were returning home to a country halfhearted in its welcome. Racial unrest released passions long suppressed, and America had lived through long, hot summers when blocks of cities were burned in protest of neglect and poverty.

Vonette felt burdened with concern about the moral condition of America. "We were falling apart at the seams in our decadence," she says. She dreamed of a grassroots kind of evangelism, one that would open the hearts of Americans to God's love and forgiveness. A movement that would help people understand their need of the Lord and long for repentance.

She firmly believed that women needed to get involved in their communities, to be—as Christ said—the salt and light of the world. Vonette encouraged women to make a difference, and locally they did.

In 1969 Vonette Bright was asked to speak at a special luncheon for women. She made out a form for women, suggesting ways to grow, to live out the Christian life, and to spread the gospel. She met with other women leaders to discuss and brainstorm on the concept of what women could

Special days of prayer have been a part of the United States of America since the Continental Congress. Nearly every president has called for a national day of prayer, especially if the nation was facing a crisis or a time of special concern.

❖ The Continental Congress. A special problem arose and the group couldn't come to an agreement. Benjamin Franklin is quoted as saying, "If a sparrow can't fall without God's notice, I doubt if a nation can rise without His special care."

❖ George Washington called for a day of prayer.

❖ Abraham Lincoln set aside April 30 as a day of "humiliation and fasting." This was a day for humbling the heart before God during the Civil War and asking for His divine intervention.

❖ Nearly every U.S. president has acknowledged the need for prayer and set aside a certain day. But there was a time when it seemed to be lost. A time when many years went by without public recognition that America needed to spend time on its knees.

❖ Senator Carlson, of Kansas, sponsored a bill stating that the president of the United States should set aside "an appropriate day" each year for prayer. This was voted into law under President Harry Truman. It was to be a day other than Sunday, and President Truman set the Day of Prayer on the Fourth of July or another holiday. It was not announced in advance.

❖ President Eisenhower recognized the importance of setting aside a day to recognize the nation's need for prayer. He wanted it to be observed by the government as well as the general population. Eisenhower himself went to the National Presbyterian Church in Bethesda, Maryland, on the Day of Prayer. He was surprised and disappointed that few people observed it.

❖ The Senate chaplain said that he doubted a day of prayer would ever really be observed if it was not set apart as a permanent date.

do. It was almost revolutionary. Ruth Graham suggested that women everywhere should be mobilized to pray. But how could that be accomplished? They didn't know, but they came together and sought God for an answer.

Following this meeting Vonette was invited to speak on the subject of prayer. She used Acts 4:16-32 as her theme. The prayer of Peter and John, just released from prison, became a challenge and a goal. For nearly 2,000 years before, like Vonette, Peter and John had been concerned about the decadence of their day. They prayed for unity, to be able to pray and work with one heart and mind. And they prayed for boldness and for power.

Unity. Boldness. Power for the Lord. It was specific, and it was strategic. It was prompted by the voice of God, and these women knew He was leading them, just as He had led the apostles in the early church.

Their goal began to take shape. They developed a manual and began to teach women the principles of prayer. They called their project "The Great Commission Prayer Crusade."

Ruth Graham, Vonette Bright, and others led in a prayer event in the Los Angeles Sports Arena. Fifteen thousand women with a vision for the need of prayer attended, and a movement was born. Prayer rallies, prayer conferences, prayer breakfasts, and prayer meetings were held in all the major cities of the United States.

But God wasn't limiting His power to only this group. He was speaking to many other groups, and in 1974 Vonette brought the leaders of the different organizations together in Washington, D.C., for a summit on prayer.

Prayer teams became a vital part of the follow-up of new believers after Billy Graham crusades. Christian organizations such as World Vision began to appoint staff members for the work of prayer. Before long more than 70 organizations were known for their work in encouraging prayer. Representatives from these groups were invited to the Christian Embassy (a ministry of Campus Crusade for Christ) in Washington, D.C. Their common passion: to promote prayer and revival.

In 1981 Vonette participated in the North American Festival of Evangelism in Kansas City. She conducted prayer workshops that taught how to plan prayer support for evangelism.

The prayer committee met in July of 1981 to determine what their next move should be. Vonette had been involved with two national days of prayer that President Carter had supported, and she was beginning to see its potential. But they'd both been announced just two weeks before the date, and that didn't allow time for planning or even for getting the news out to everyone across America.

For several years the National Day of Prayer had been unofficially on the first Thursday in May, so it was beginning to be established in some places. But for most of America, it hadn't caught on.

Then an interested businessman called Vonette. She has always felt God led him to do so for he'd been watching the development of the National Day of Prayer and saw potential for something significant. "There is great opportunity to call the people of America to prayer," he said. "It can be very meaningful and effective. But it will never happen until we have a permanent date."

A permanent date was far more than their committee could accomplish. It would take diligent work, commitment, and prayer and more prayer. Congress would have to vote it, and the president of the United States would need to sign it into law.

In 1982 the original prayer committee took up the challenge and began working with denominational leaders. They made contacts in the House, the Senate, and the White House.

They were treated royally in Washington and met with senators who were active in the prayer breakfast movement. The lawmakers saw the value of the cause they championed, and made the committee official. In 1983 the committee members worked to inform and unite those who were sympathetic to a permanent date for a national day of prayer. Excitement spread across the nation as word began to spread. Churches began to appoint prayer coordinators for planned, specific prayer emphasis in their parishes. Pastors became involved.

Several years passed. By now the National Day of Prayer (NDOP) had been on the first Thursday in May for seven consecutive years. The committee knew it would take support from the right people in Washington to make it permanent, and that wasn't happening. Vonette had been working with President Reagan and knew him as an ally. But this was the end of his second term—1988—and if it was going to happen, it had to happen now.

Then Senator Strom Thurmond volunteered to sponsor the bill. One might think that from then on it would have been fairly uncomplicated to get the bill through Congress and signed into law, but it wasn't. Instead, things grew more difficult. But God had His plans in place.

As it happened, Vonette's son, Brad, was working on

the staff of Senator Bill Armstrong. Vonette asked Brad to outline the steps necessary to get a bill introduced. She followed his instructions exactly.

The committee and many others were praying intensely at each step of the process. Vonette went to Ohio representative Tony Hall and asked for his help. He was a new Christian, but was too busy to take it on. She tried others, to no avail.

But Vonette Bright had a vision in her heart and would not give up. She was inspired by a God who is patient and kind and doesn't give up on His children. He tells us in Deuteronomy 4:4 and 10:20 that we should *hold Him fast.* No matter how bleak the situation may appear, to look above the circumstances to a God who can change the circumstances. No matter what, to keep on, to hold on.

Chuck Fullmore's song says it so well:

"Hold on a little longer, my friend.
Hold on a little longer and don't give in.
Jesus has promised His love to the end.
Hold on a little longer, my friend."

Our faith may be tested by dead ends and seeming failures, but it grows stronger as we wait for Him. God has promised that those who wait on the Lord shall renew their strength (Isaiah 40:31). He even promises that we will become stronger as we trust Him. That's worth the effort.

So Vonette held on. She wrote letters. She knocked on doors. She made uncounted phone calls, looking for more help to convince the country's lawmakers. And she prayed. No matter who was there to discourage her or to point out the futility of taking on the United States government. No matter how impossible her dream seemed to be, there was, in the words of the spiritual, "something within me":

> "There is something within me, that holdeth the reins,
> Something within me, I cannot explain.
> Something within me, I cannot explain,
> All that I know, there is something within."

And *that* kept Vonette going.

She learned that the words of Hebrews 10:23 are true: "Let us hold fast to the confession of our hope without wavering, for he who has promised is faithful" (NRSV).

She thought of Abraham Lincoln, remembering that when he was told that God was on his side replied, "That may be, but the important thing is for me to be on His side." Vonette wanted that too. She believed that God was leading and that she must be on His side, and faithful to His call.

So she continued to work and pray. One Tuesday morning while visiting on the West Coast, Vonette had a growing sense that Tony Hall was the man God had picked for the job. Rising at 4:00 a.m. to call him at home before he left for his Washington, D.C., office, she asked once again if he would help. He said yes. "I promised the Lord that if you called me one more time, I would put my efforts into this cause," he told her.

One hundred twenty-five representatives signed the bill and responded to it. Thurmond and Hall and others worked behind the scenes, explaining, teaching, lobbying, encouraging. The bill passed unanimously in both the Senate and the House. It was April 18, 1988. The bill was sent to the president to sign.

Vonette stayed with the bill constantly, to keep track of where it was in the process. President Reagan signed it on May 5, the first Thursday of that month. From then on the first

Thursday of May would be America's National Day of Prayer.

Having it as a specific, permanent day gives people all over America time to plan and motivate and come together in unity to pray for the nation and its leaders. And God has kept His hand over this work. In 1998—at its 10-year mark—Vonette Bright and the legislators who worked for it were recognized and publically appreciated for their combined efforts, under the blessing and the power of God. "The Lord is my rock, and my fortress, and my deliverer; my God, my strength, in whom I will trust; my buckler, and the horn of my salvation, and my high tower" (Ps. 18:2).

Reliving those difficult but triumphant days, Vonette can agree with Martin Luther: "A mighty fortress is my God."

My Fortress.

It's one of His names.

PROMISES

Perseverance has been defined as "courage stretched out." God calls us to a courageous and enduring faithfulness in the midst of trials.

God honors persistence in prayer (Matt. 7:7).

God never stops working in our lives (Phil. 1:6).

Those who persevere in their faith will share in heaven's riches (Heb. 3:14; Rev. 3:5; 21:7).

Chapter 11

THE DISAPPEARING PERMIT

Patsy was bewildered. This just didn't make sense. Just a few days before, she'd been given *the* document—the official residence permit from the Tanzanian government that would allow a new teacher from the United States to join the faculty at Tanzania Adventist Seminary and college near Arusha. Patsy was sure she had tucked the document in its manila envelope, and placed it carefully into a drawer in the safe and not given it another thought.

But now when a faculty member came en route to Kenya to meet the newcomer and needed to take the residence permit with him, it was gone! He told her not to worry. "I don't need to leave for Kenya until Sunday," he assured her. "I'm sure you will have found it by then."

Patsy wasn't easily comforted for she simply had no idea where it could be. Worried, she reviewed the options. It would be impossible to get another permit in time. This one had been delayed, taking six weeks to arrive. She had to find the permit before Sunday.

Praying as she searched, she carefully and methodically went through everything she could think of. First, of course,

78

the safe. Then drawers and cabinets. Files. Any place, she reasoned, that she remotely might have absentmindedly put it. She *knew* she had put it in the safe—she remembered placing it there. Oh, what could have happened to it?

Her thoughts turned toward God all during the day. Praying for wisdom, for faith to trust Him. Praying for His will to be done in everything—even with the missing document. She thought of the many times that God had shown His faithfulness and presence during nearly 20 years when she and her husband, Joe, had been missionaries in Tanzania. They had seen God do some amazing things in answer to prayer.

Patsy remembered the time about 10 years earlier when they'd had a head-on collision with evil. It happened on a Sabbath morning as they were preparing breakfast and getting ready for church. Two men came to their door. Pretending to have car trouble and needing to use the phone, they'd forced their way into the house. They were rough and harsh, and seemed bent on a mission of evil. Patsy and Joe hardly breathed as the men went through the kitchen, where a large butcher knife lay on the counter. *But the men didn't seem to notice it, and their lives had been spared.*

There was something else she would never forget from that day. They'd had a large amount of money in the house. It was unusual, but it was there, waiting until they could take it to the bank. God had blinded the eyes of the thieves, and they didn't see it.

It had been a frightening experience, and when the men finally left, they fell on their knees and thanked God for His protection. They could not mistake His power in their time of desperate need.

So now in this simple yet complex situation, Patsy again turned to God. Of course, she kept on searching for the document, as well as praying. The days passed. Friday arrived. Time was running out.

Despite the emergency, Patsy's faith gave her a quietness and calm she could not explain. Faith in God brings peace of mind because we know that we belong to Him and He is in charge, even when we cannot understand. And faith in God leads us to trust Him with our lives. Faith is not just an act of our mind—it taps us into the very resources that God has for us, and we are able to live in an entirely new way.

That Friday night she had another special conversation with God. "Lord, You know exactly where that paper is," she said. "You know that I have tried to be as careful as possible and I've looked through the entire office. There is nothing else I can do. You have promised to be with me and never forsake me [Heb. 13:5]. You promised to give me wisdom [James 1:5]. So now I'm trusting You for guidance."

She had a special peace as she drifted off to sleep. What a blessed assurance is His presence with us.

In the middle of the night she sat straight up in bed, wide awake with only one thought in mind. She didn't hear an audible voice, but it was unmistakably clear. *Pull out the entire drawer and look under it. The envelope has fallen out of the drawer into the space at the back. It's totally concealed, under the drawer.*

She hadn't thought of that before because she had assumed that the drawer was entirely sealed, and didn't know of any space beneath it. But the next morning, after a good night's rest, she told Joe, "I know where that envelope is."

"You do? Where?"

Patsy explained the thought that had come to her during the night.

It was now Sabbath morning, and they were at home. The safe was in the union office there in Arusha. They went through their usual Sabbath routines of church, lunch, and afternoon activities. Joe was eager to help her in any way he could, and willing to go to the office to check on the envelope. But Patsy felt no hurry to retrieve it. God had given her a special peace.

That evening she and Joe walked to the office building across the compound from their home. The safe was small and it looked impossible to remove the drawer, but at last Joe was able to take it out. The brown manila folder lay in the space under the drawer. It would never have been found without removing the drawer. And that would never have occurred to Patsy, for she didn't know how the safe was constructed.

When the driver came to get the vital document the next day, she gave it to him with a smile and a heart full of gratitude to the Lord who had done this for her. To Patsy and Joe this was another message of God's concern, His nearness, His love, His faithfulness, and His presence with them.

David tells us in Psalm 46:1, "God is our refuge and strength, a very *present* help in trouble" (NRSV). It's true. Our God is near.

Jehovah Shammah, the Lord who is present.

It's one of His names.

PROMISES

"Now faith is being sure of what we hope for and certain of what we do not see" (Heb. 11:1, NIV).

"May the God of hope fill you with all joy and peace as you trust in him, so that you may overflow with hope by the power of the Holy Spirit" (Rom. 15:13, NIV).

Chapter 12

"HE FIRST SETS
HIS PEOPLE TO PRAY"

Radio Good News is a small community radio station covering south Johannesburg, South Africa. It's a Christian station broadcasting music, information for healthful living, some religious programming, and topics of community interest. When the time came for its license to be renewed, Marie Lello, an Adventist layperson and manager of the station, faced a problem.

Marie needed 5,000 rand (approximately US$1,000), and she needed it immediately. Two costs faced her: the license renewal for Radio Good News and payroll for her staff of six. She could manage to pay one. She didn't have the money for both.

First there was the application fee of 3,000 rand (approximately US$600). In addition to that unexpected cost, the license application required a radiation hazard study. That would cost another 1,000 rand—again, unexpected, and surely not in the bank.

Then there was the cost of printing, for some parts of the application for license renewal had to be in color. Collating and binding the applications added another 1,000 rand. Each application was nearly an inch thick, and the government required 25 copies.

Radio Good News is supported solely by listener donations and inevitably the support is there. Day after day Marie and her staff watched the Lord answer needs as they arose. And so Marie prayed for wisdom. Constantly.

She had no choice but to go forward for without a license they'd be out of business. She asked her accountant to write the checks for the license application. His look said, "This is ridiculous!" If the money was spent, it would be impossible to meet other pressing obligations. Reluctantly he carried out her wishes.

Keep in mind that Marie had continually lifted this problem before the Lord. She didn't want to run ahead of Him, but then, she didn't want to lag behind. And once she made the decision to apply for the license renewal, she had peace. Her only concern was to be sure that the forms were filled out correctly. And so she worked hard and carefully, depending upon God at each step. Even as she worked, she prayed earnestly that God would fulfill His promise to supply her needs—the money for payroll and other obligations. Eagerly she checked each envelope that came through the mail, somehow expecting that God would answer. Each time she was disappointed. The money didn't come.

On Friday she delivered the three checks and took the applications to the office of licensure. Sabbath morning she went to church, at peace. She asked God for a special sense of His nearness that day that she might find some encouragement. She also asked that He might send her some affirmation that her act of faith was pleasing to Him.

At the church each member had a small pigeonhole, a

little cubicle, where church bulletins, newsletters, church journals, and other information was distributed. Entering the church, Marie checked her cubicle as usual. With the other materials in the box she found an envelope with her name on it in care of Radio Good News. Opening the envelope, she found a check for exactly 5,000 rand—the exact amount so desperately needed. Marie stood there, weeping with relief and joy as she realized how dramatically God had worked, and just in time.

There was no signature on the cashier's check, so she contacted the bank, wanting to thank the donor. "The donor prefers to remain anonymous," the official told her, and promised to convey her thanks.

Marie's heart sang as she related her story to us, and her faith is stronger now than ever. She *knows* God hears and answers prayer.

Many years ago five ministerial students visited London, thrilled at the opportunity to hear some well-known preachers. The sun was hot as they waited for the doors to Spurgeon's Tabernacle to open, the church of one of London's most famous preachers. Then a stranger approached and asked an odd question. "While you're waiting, would you like to see the heating apparatus of the church?"

That was the last thing they had in mind on a boiling July day, but they followed as the man led them down some steps to a basement door. Pushing open the door, he reverently whispered, "There is our heating apparatus."

The young interns saw 700 people bowed in prayer, asking for God's blessing on the upcoming service. Their unknown guide was Spurgeon himself. His ministry was powerful because of prayer.

The same power "lights" churches today. I visited some of them recently in New York City.

"Auntie Jessie" met my taxi as it pulled up to the North Bronx church that Friday evening. She helped me with my luggage, then took me into the church. It was full. It had been full every night that week as members and their friends had come together for a special week of Bible study and prayer. That particular evening a prayer service was planned to last till midnight. However, it was some time beyond midnight when it ended. I felt a sense of urgency and intensity during those hours of prayer. God's presence was there.

One after another stood to thank God for answers to prayer, and for the blessings they'd enjoyed that week. It was thrilling to see their radiant faces as they thanked the Lord for His personal love. No one seemed concerned about the lateness of the hour. No one seemed to notice. It was simply a time of worship.

Deuteronomy 28:12 and 13 offers specific encouragement to God's children: "I will open my good treasure to you and bless all the work of your hand . . . you will lend to many nations, but you will not borrow. I will make you the head and not the tail. You will be above only, and you will not be beneath" (paraphrase).

Specific promises to God's children who are obedient

to His commandments. These promises had come to life in the experiences of those kneeling in that church. I was thrilled to hear their stories for these centuries-old verses had been fulfilled anew.

Early the next morning we began making the whirlwind rounds from church to church . . . to church. Some had designated that Sabbath as a day of prayer and fasting. We visited and prayed with 19 different church groups—Hispanic, French, Jamaican, and African-American.

It was a wonderful privilege to see God working in those churches. To see the hunger and desire for prayer. The congregations varied in size from just a few to thousands. But everywhere we went we found people of God whose lives were being changed by prayer.

They prayed for more than financial or physical needs. They prayed for renewal, for healing between the races, and for power to share God's love and grace with those who have no hope. And they prayed because they knew that prayer is being with God.

A capstone for the weekend was the all-night prayer service held Saturday night at the Northeastern Conference office in Queens, New York. It was well attended all night long. Many shared deep personal testimonies. They lifted each other up in heartfelt prayers; they interceded for their pastors and for their city.

Vanessa Jones, a graduate student and church member for only two years, had something on her heart that blessed us all. She'd been reading *The Southern Work,* by Ellen White. It painted a vivid picture of life and culture throughout the United States around the time of the Civil War.

At that time it was not only unpopular for a White person to minister to someone of "the colored race" (as Blacks were called); it was downright dangerous. Feelings were strong, and those who risked their lives to take the gospel to former slaves were often ostracized from their families. Some even suffered injury or death.

"What are we doing to pay them back?" Vanessa asked. "They sacrificed for us. Couldn't we do something to help them now?"

Several people responded and ideas were discussed. Then they prayed, asking God for healing and for wisdom to find creative ways to help White persons who do not know Christ.

The holy hours passed. The all-night service became a time for affirmations, blessings, and prayers for God's empowerment.

"When God wants to do a great work," Spurgeon said, "He first sets His people to pray."

But this was New York. This was where the term *cocooning* was born. Where people go home from work and lock themselves in their houses and apartments. This is the city where people fear to go out at night. Yet here were people from all over the city, coming together for prayer until after midnight. And coming again on the following night, to pray until dawn. Even in New York City? Yes! God's people are still finding the same "heating apparatus" and power available to individuals, to families, and to churches. The Christian community is growing in New York. In Brooklyn alone there are more than 100 Seventh-day Adventist churches.

God has set His people in New York City to pray, and in response He is doing a great work there.

El Shaddai, Almighty God.
It's one of His names.

PROMISES

When God wants to do a great work, He first sets His people to pray.

"For in [Christ] every one of God's promises is a 'yes'" (2 Cor. 1:20, NRSV).

"Then many will give thanks on our behalf for the gracious favor granted us in answer to the prayers of many" (2 Cor. 1:11, NIV).

Chapter 13

"Yes, Lord. Yes!"

It was a sunny Sabbath morning in Kettering, Ohio, when Hazel met Chris and her husband. She met him first, and he quietly told her that while he was a member of the Adventist Church his wife was not. He hoped Hazel could get acquainted with her.

After church was over, Hazel met Chris, a delightful Christian woman of a different faith. Hazel asked Chris about her interests and told her that she led out in a women's Bible study group. She gave Chris her phone number, inviting her to call if she'd like to join the Bible study group.

Chris called a few days later with some excitement and thoughts of her own. "I wondered if you would come to my house and lead a group for my neighbors and friends. I have a large house with plenty of room, and the others don't work. We'll arrange a time around their tennis or golf. I'd love to have you come," she said, but felt she should make something clear. "I'm a Lutheran, and I have to ask you not to try to make me a Seventh-day Adventist. My husband understands. He comes to church with me on Sundays and I go with him on Saturdays."

Hazel promised her that she would not try to make her an Adventist. But she prayed daily for Chris and the others.

Weeks passed. The Bible study in Chris's home was well attended. But one particular day found Hazel in a quandary. On the pastoral staff of the Kettering church she sometimes faced difficult situations, but this time it seemed different. The next day Chris and her neighbors would be studying John 13—the story of the Last Supper before Christ's death.

As Hazel had studied and prayed for this group, she kept thinking of how closely the group had bonded together. These friends loved each other and were coming to know Jesus, too. Hazel felt that God wanted them to experience the full message of John 13. She longed to introduce them to the entire Communion service, but she had promised Chris that she would not impose the unique beliefs of Seventh-day Adventists on the group.

And yet, the blessing they were missing . . .

"It is by receiving the life for us poured out on Calvary's cross, that we can live the life of holiness. . . . As faith contemplates our Lord's great sacrifice, the soul assimilates the spiritual life of Christ. That soul will receive spiritual strength from every Communion. The service forms a living connection by which the believer is bound up with Christ, and thus bound up with the Father" (*The Desire of Ages,* pp. 660, 661).

And so studying the beautiful story of the Last Supper, the thought of the ordinance of foot washing weighed heavily on her mind. "Lord," she prayed, "You know I promised Chris I wouldn't try to make her an Adventist. And I don't think she would trust me if I suggest that the group observe the whole Communion service. But Lord, it says that You washed Your disciples' feet because You wanted to show them Your love, and these young ladies love You so much. I believe they need to experience a new level of Your presence and forgiveness. But I can't go back on my word to Chris. If You want me to do this, I'll do it. But You'll have to make it obvious. If You do, I'll obey."

She didn't understand exactly how God was leading, but after praying she had peace. That's all she did. Prayed and put her dilemma in God's hands. The next morning on her way to Chris's home she stopped at a supermarket where Jewish foods are available and bought some unleavened bread and grape juice. Now she had the symbol of Christ's broken body and His blood. She was ready.

No one else had arrived when she got there. Walking into Chris's beautiful home, she was met by the smiling host, who quickly pulled her into the pantry. "Hazel, I want to show you something," she said with a little grin. "As I was praying and studying our Bible passage this week, I kept thinking about the way you do the Communion service at your church. I have thought it was an awesome experience, and have wished that all of us could do it together. Here in my home. I know that none of my friends have ever had that experience."

Hazel could hardly believe her ears—or her eyes. "So I called your church," Chris went on, "and asked them if I could borrow enough basins and towels for our group. When I drove over to get them, everyone was so helpful. I just told them that I was in Hazel's Bible study group and we were studying the Communion chapter in John 13."

And there, neatly stacked on a shelf in the pantry, were

12 basins and 12 towels. *God, You really did something amazing this time!* Hazel thought.

Then she told Chris that she'd brought unleavened bread and grape juice, so now they had everything they needed. The two friends wept for joy as they saw how God had met them in such a specific way, in answer to their separate prayers.

Then the women started arriving, greeting each other. Talking, laughing together as they shared hot drinks and the latest news. Soon it was time for the Bible study and they were eager to get into it.

They prayed first, asking God to send His Holy Spirit to their group. Thanking God for His mercy and forgiveness, for His presence in their lives.

They began by reading John 13:1 and noted that Christ was almost at the end of His work on earth and wanted to show His disciples the full extent of His love.

How did He choose to do so? What method did Christ use?

The story continued with the evening meal of unleavened bread, the Passover meal. The devil had already prompted Judas to betray Christ (verse 2), but Jesus knew that God was in control. And to provide a living illustration that He came to serve humanity, Christ did something shocking. He wrapped a towel around his waist, poured water into a basin, and one by one began to wash the dusty feet of His disciples.

This was the job of a servant.

The roads they walked were not paved. The sandals they wore left most of their feet bare. It was a courtesy for a host to provide a servant to wash the feet of his guests.

But no servant was available.

Not one of the men around the table would have humiliated himself to perform the task.

The women enjoyed a lively discussion of these verses. They discussed the meaning of Christ's reply to Peter who objected to His leader stooping to wash his feet (verses 6-8).

It was a thrill to look at a passage in depth, to listen for the small voice of the Holy Spirit as He led them to deeper understanding of Christ's sacrifice and the deep meaning in being one of His disciples..

Then Hazel looked around the group. "Chris and I thought you might like to experience the foot washing and the communion service here this morning," she said. And she explained how they might serve each other.

Chris went to the pantry and brought out the basins and towels. The women solemnly knelt before one another. They slipped their bare feet into the warm water. They rubbed dry the wet feet of their friends with their toweled hands.

"I have attended and participated in Communion services all my life," Hazel told me, "but never have I seen the heartfelt joy and cleansing that I saw that morning, as those precious new children of God washed each other's feet, asking for forgiveness and praying for each other.

"It was a precious time. I felt the angels close to us."

Afterward they continued through the chapter, discussing the last meal Christ ate with His disciples. Then Hazel brought out the unleavened bread and grape juice and the women ate and drank of the symbol of Christ's broken body and His blood.

It was a solemn time, a time of special awareness that

Jesus had done something out of the ordinary for them. That He had actually touched their lives as they sat in that room that morning, and that He longed for them to enjoy their "newness" in Him.

"Hazel, could we go to the piano and sing 'What a Friend We Have in Jesus?'" someone asked. As they did they felt a new depth of meaning in the words.

Hazel slipped over to one of her friends, a woman whose parents had been praying that she would return to the church of her childhood. She said, "Sue, don't you think it's time to come home?"

Sue didn't hesitate. She hugged Hazel and whispered, "Thank you." Then she said, "Will you come over to my home and study with my husband and me? I think we're both ready."

What a morning!

Hazel drove home with a light and happy heart. "Lord, how did You do *that?*" she asked.

In the weeks that passed Sue and her husband drew closer to the Lord. And then they were ready for baptism.

And Chris. Hazel had promised not to try to make an Adventist out of her, and she didn't. But God had a plan of His own. And Hazel rejoiced with Chris and her husband the day she publicly confirmed her commitment to God and was baptized into the Seventh-day Adventist Church. Our God is a God of surprises. His answers are creative; always better than anything we could plan. And He wants us to know daily that He is the one who saves us.

Jesus, our Saviour.

It's one of His names.

PROMISES

"You shall call His name Jesus, for He will save His people from their sins" (Matt. 1:21).

"I will instruct you and teach you in the way you should go;
I will counsel you and watch over you.
Do not be like the horse or the mule,
which have no understanding but must be controlled
by bit and bridle or they will not come to you. . . .

"Rejoice in the Lord and be glad, you righteous;
sing, all you who are upright in heart!"
(Ps. 32:8-11, NIV).

" 'For I know the plans I have for you,' " declares the Lord, 'plans to prosper you and not to harm you, plans to give you hope and a future' " (Jer. 29:11, NIV).

God wants His children to obey Him with an obedience motivated by trust and love. This frees us to enjoy life in the fullest, as God intended us to do. Though obedience may not make sense from a human point of view, it always brings blessing, joy, and peace.

Chapter 14

LORD

OF THE IMPOSSIBLE

Come walk with me into the prestigious Russell Senate Office Building in America's Capitol, in Washington, D.C. Look up at the high ceilings and stately columns. You'll be awed, as I am each time I experience its grandeur.

Come, we'll go through the security check, take the elevator to the third floor, and walk down that magnificent corridor with its 18-foot ceilings. We're passing Senator Ted Kennedy's office right now. The door is open, and people are busy in the outer office.

We keep going to the far end of the corridor. We're at the rotunda, a vast circle of majestic marble columns. If we walk over to the marble barricade we can look down to the first floor below. The beauty is awesome. I'm always impressed with the architecture as well as the rich history in this place.

But let's keep walking around the columns. I always think of them as giant carved sentinels. They span three or more floors, you know, standing proudly in their white splendor. We'll go on to the far end of the building. There on either side of the window that frames the Capitol are the offices of the chaplain of the United States Senate.

Though I am impressed by the architecture, now a different kind of emotion wells up as I meet Patricia, Heather, and then Lloyd Ogilvie, the chaplain. Maybe the awe is still there, because God is using Ogilvie and his assistants in an exceptional way. It's a busy office, of course, but it also holds an aura of calm. Ogilvie and his staff believe they've been appointed by God to serve His people on Capitol Hill.

Among other responsibilities, they plan special times for various groups to meet for prayer and Bible study. I have visited the office a few times and always come away inspired. On this occasion I had an interview with Ogilvie for a short video on prayer.

"When in your life and ministry did prayer become the great priority that it is today?" I asked.

"Ruthie, that is a personal and profound question," he said with a smile. "It happened when I was in Edinburg, Scotland, for graduate studies. I'd already been in the ministry for eight years."

He went on to tell the experience he also describes in his book *Loved and Forgiven*. I'm going to let him tell you in his own words:

"It happened when I realized that I had a purpose without power. After a few years in the ministry I was exhausted and frustrated. My preaching was biblically oriented and Christ-centered, but few lives were moved or changed. My church was well organized and highly programmed, but there was neither love nor joy among the people. Most of all, I was aware that something was wrong—missing—lacking. Years of theological education and biblical exposition had hit wide of the mark of the most crucial truth the Word contained. In my discouragement and despair I asked Christ to tell me what was wrong.

"My personal devotions, kept regularly but fruitlessly up to that time, were in John and Colossians. One day I was led to read Christ's promise that He could make His home with us (see John 14:23). Then I read these words in Colossians: "Christ in you, the hope of glory" (Col. 1:27). They sounded like a trumpet blast.

" 'That's it!' I said. I had tried to follow Christ to the best of *my* ability. I was a man 'in Christ' as a recipient of the gift of His death and resurrection for me. I knew that I was forgiven. But now I was stunned intellectually with a truth I had missed. I was stirred emotionally by a power I had not appropriated. And most of all, I was startled by a vision of what the Christian was meant to be. The indwelling place of Christ, the glorious riverbed of the flowing stream of the living Lord!

"I got on my knees. 'Lord, I've missed the secret. I have been ministering for You and have not allowed You to work through me. Come live Your life in me. Love through me; forgive through me; suffer for the estranged through me; continue fresh realizations of Calvary everywhere about me.'

"The result of that prayer is that I discovered that guidance is not something I go to Christ to receive, but something He signals from within my mind and spirit.

"Each person I met or worked with gave me a fresh opportunity to let go and allow Christ to speak and love through me. I found, and continually rediscover now, that my task is only to pray for openness to let Him through and then to marvel at what He says and does.

"Problems and difficulties are gifts for new levels of depth in experiencing the limitless adequacy of what Christ can do. What a relief it is to no longer feel that I have to find answers and solve problems to please or placate Him. He is at work in me.

"I know that as surely as I feel my heart beat and my lungs breathe. But don't misread my enthusiasm. I am not suggesting that there has been no pain or suffering. The difference is that there is less of the excruciating distress caused by my previous resistance to Him and more of the realization that the difficulties of living are the focus of the next phase of the penetration of the power of the cross."*

Ogilvie has written more than 44 books, each one packed with encouragement from Scripture. We talked briefly about some of his books, and about his dependence on prayer. This man has a profound trust in God, and prayer is a singular priority in his life.

Listen to what he says in *Lord of the Impossible*. He asks a crucial question, and I hear it as a challenge to me and to you.

"What are you attempting that you cannot accomplish without an intervention from the Lord? That's a question I've asked others and myself for years. Most of us live our lives within the narrow limits of what we can do on our own strength and talents. We keep life carefully constricted inside the boundaries of what we are sure we can handle by ourselves. In reality, we don't need God. Our fear of risk keeps us away from anything we cannot control or do with our own ability.

"At the same time we are surrounded with problems, challenges, and opportunities. We tackle the things that can't be avoided. Our vision of what can happen is usually calculated on what we are able to do with our own resources and experience. When we do ask for God's help, our prayers are often for His power to do what we think is best. He is gracious to respond, and our Christianity settles into the set of self-determined possibilities."

He continued that after sharing these thoughts with his congregation one worship service, they took a prolonged time for prayer. He asked each person to think about his or her life on several levels. He guided them to reflect on the unlimited power of God. Then he asked:

"What would we dare to attempt if we were sure that the Lord would intervene to help us? What have we avoided by saying, 'Why, that's impossible'? Where have we stepped back from involvement in something that *we couldn't do by ourselves?*"

He asked them to picture the impossible person, the difficult relationship, limitation, illness, crisis, or assignment that they had kept at arm's length because they wanted to keep life "safe" and risk-free. Then they dared to ask God to give them a picture of how they would live if He were to unleash the power that is revealed in the book of Acts.

"To blast the cap off our limited perception of what is possible we read John 14:12-14, 'Most assuredly, I say to you, he who believes in Me, the works that I do he will do also; and greater works than these he will do, because I go to My Father. And whatever you ask in My name, that I will do, that the Father may be glorified in the Son. If you ask anything in My name, I will do it' [NKJV]."

After the congregation had prayerfully reached that promise, the atmosphere in the sanctuary was electric.

"Had the same power to love, forgive, heal, reconcile, and take up our cross of obedience been given to us?" Ogilvie went on. "Yes! And more than that, we have been called to do the thing Jesus of Nazareth could not do when He spoke this promise prior to the Crucifixion, Resurrection, and Pentecost—introduce people to Him as the living, victorious Lord!

"Whom do we need to risk time and costly caring to communicate Jesus' love? What opportunities for service in the social sickness of our community are we carefully avoiding? What goals for our families, our work, our church, does the Lord want us to risk our security to attempt?"

After this incisive inventory, Ogilvie asked the congregation to place their open hands before them. Then they symbolically placed in their hands the person, situation, problem, or action on which they would focus their prayers. He asked each one to consider what God was guiding them to do, or to be, or to attempt—all impossible without His intervention and power. Then when they were ready, they were invited to lift their hands filled with "impossibilities" in expectant surrender to the Lord.

"Looking out over the congregation," he wrote, "I saw hands go up, slowly at first, and then with vigor, until almost every person sat with arms uplifted, hands open, releasing the God-guided and focused impossibilities to Him. The closing hymn shook the rafters."

Oswald Chambers says that our impossibilities "provide a platform for the display of His almighty grace and power." The God of power, who loves and forgives us, is the great I AM who stands behind His promises.

When Moses asked God to tell him His name, He told

Moses, "Say to the Israelites: 'I AM has sent me to you'" (Ex. 3:14, NIV).

I AM everything you need Me to be. And with Me, nothing is impossible.

The great I AM. It's one of His names.

Loved and Forgiven, pp. 54-56.

Chapter 15

ATTITUDES
AND ANGELS

"What has God done for you in the past 24 hours that shows you that He loves you?" my friend Ginger Church asked the group attending her afternoon seminar at the Washington Conference camp meeting. Ginger, in periodical marketing at the Review and Herald Publishing Association, enjoys starting her seminars with a personal touch. "You have three minutes to share this with the person sitting next to you."

The room began to buzz with voices. When the time was up Ginger asked if anyone had heard a story they would like to share?

Immediately a man raised his hand. "I know you asked for us to tell what the other person told us," he said, "but in this case I think the woman next to me should tell it herself."

Well, OK. Ginger's flexible. With a smile, she invited the woman to speak.

Mercene stood up. "Last night after the evening meeting the speaker invited anyone who wanted to remain after the service to stay for a time of praise and sharing. The young man seated next to me stood and said, 'I'm not an

Adventist, but I've come here to find the Lord. You see, I have AIDS and I'm dying.'"

At that confession Mercene had quietly slipped into an empty place two seats over. She wanted to put a little distance between herself and the man with AIDS. As he continued talking, Mercene recounted how she had looked back at him, and to her amazement had seen *two tall, shining angels, one on each side of the young man!*

"I felt humbled and ashamed," Mercene told the group. "I felt as though God were saying to me, 'I love him and died for him. You should love him too.'

"Silently I slipped back to the seat next to him. Tapping on his arm, I asked, 'Could I give you a hug?' Then I told him, in awe, 'Did you know that you had two large and shining angels standing by your side as you spoke? I *know* God is with you and He loves you.'"

The woman and the young man had hugged each other, both of them weeping at the miracles that had happened. First, the miracle of changing Mercene's heart. Then the miracle of making visible two ambassadors from heaven for a young man who needed to know that God loved him.

Recently Ginger told me another story about the God who cares. As a young wife and mother Ginger was sometimes frustrated and lonely. Her husband often traveled and needed the car for his work. She felt trapped and friendless. Her only companions were their two young sons. One day one of the boys asked her, "Mommy, why do you frown so much?" She was shocked at his question, but realized it was true.

"I had a sad attitude," Ginger told me. "I didn't want that. I asked the Lord to please change me. I asked Him to let me be known as 'the woman who smiles.'

"Not long after that prayer I answered a knock at my door. A pleasant woman stood there with an unusual message. She told me that I'd been chosen as an Avon representative.

" 'Well, I don't want to be an Avon representative,' I told her. I had no intention of ever selling Avon. I'd never sold anything, and had no desire to try.

"She explained that it would cost only $25 for me to get started, and reminded me that I had been *chosen.* She left the materials with me and encouraged me to talk it over with my husband, saying she'd be back in a week for my answer.

"I was completely unconvinced, but my husband, Dennis, surprised me when I discussed it with him. 'I think this is exactly what you need,' he said. 'This will get you out of the house and give you something to do. You'll have lots of opportunities to meet people, and I think you'd like that. I hope you'll do it.'

"What a shock! I wasn't ready for my husband's response. Maybe this was something I really was supposed to do. So with a halfhearted commitment I accepted the territory around my home she had offered me. It didn't take long for me to realize that I liked it! Dennis was right. Going out and meeting people gave me a new vision. It gave me circles of friends, people to serve.

"But the most curious part of this is that I was never able to find the woman who came to my home to tell me that I'd been *chosen.* I was never able to learn her name or address, even though I inquired at the Avon headquarters for my area. I am convinced that God sent His angel as an Avon representative to rescue me from myself."

Just think of our all-loving, all-powerful, wonderful God. Stooping down to earth and answering the heartfelt cry of a lonely young mother. Sending her a job she wasn't looking for!

"Before you call I will answer," God tells us. Ginger knows that first-hand.

God's ways are often beyond our human understanding, and every now and then He throws in something so surprising that it takes our breath away. In Penny's story, that's what happened to Louise a few years ago.

It was a typical Michigan winter morning. Several inches of snow lay on the ground, and the sky was overcast. Snowplows had cleaned the streets, and people had shoveled their sidewalks. A brisk wind built snowdrifts everywhere.

Louise, a middle-aged woman, wanted to go to the factory where she worked to get her paycheck, and asked her husband to take her. Though she didn't drive, it usually wasn't a problem. But for whatever reason, Al didn't want to take her today. Didn't know why she couldn't wait till tomorrow, and said so. But Louise wanted her paycheck. She needed it, and so she decided to go get it herself.

They lived about a mile from the Simplicity Pattern Company where she worked, and she'd walked it often. With a mumbled "I'm going after it myself" Louise put on her coat, wrapped a scarf around her neck, and went out the door.

It was a quick walk there—first down two long blocks that ran alongside the cemetery. Then she turned right and headed toward the factory. She enjoyed the crisp air and the solitude. She went inside, got her check, and headed out again. The wall clock said 1:05.

It was growing colder and she felt chilled, so decided to take a shortcut through the cemetery on her way home. It was a large cemetery, surrounded by a high fence. But a gate near her street was always open, and as the wind was whipping up, she decided she'd better get home as quickly as possible.

But with the wind came snow. Hard pellets blew horizontally and stung her face and her bare legs beneath her coat. Good thing she was taking the shortcut, she reasoned. The snow quickly turned into a blizzard. It was hard to see, but she picked her way through the narrow lanes among the tombstones.

It was slow going. Every step was an effort. But she finally saw the fence. Almost home. "Thank You, Jesus. Thank You."

But no. Waist-high snow had drifted against the fence. She pushed through it, trying to reach the gate. But it was impossible. The snow was too deep. The gate wouldn't budge. Disheartened, Louise turned around and began to retrace her steps. She had in mind to go to another gate a little distance up the cemetery roadway. It would save precious time and energy not to go all the way back to the main city road.

Chilled to the bone, she bent against the wind. It was so hard to see. She felt her way through the tombstones, stopping often to figure out where she was. She had no real sense of the passing of time, but suddenly realized it was beginning to get dusk. *Oh, no. The caretaker will lock the gates, and then I'll never get out of here*, she thought desperately. *I'll be locked in here all night long.*

She sensed rather than saw the old pickup pull up

ATTITUDES AND ANGELS

alongside her. The driver leaned across and opened the passenger door. "Get in," he told her. "You're about to freeze to death."

"I'm on my way home," Louise explained. "I thought I'd go through the gate, but it's drifted shut. I couldn't get it open."

"Yes, I know," the man said. "Get on in. My boss sent me to get you. We've been watching you wander around here all afternoon."

It took some effort to climb into the truck, but she obeyed. She was struck by the man's eyes and kind face. "Put your legs up on the seat and get warm," he instructed. "Just look at them. A few more minutes and you could have frozen to death. You don't know just how cold you are."

Louise obeyed, suddenly realizing that she was numb with cold. Her legs were a strange mottled color, and it was hard to move. But the truck was warm and comforting, and needle pricks danced across her legs as the heat began to penetrate. She didn't want to be any trouble. "I live right across the way," she told her escort, "but you'll need to go outside on the main street and—"

"I know where you live," he said gently. "I've seen you walk through the cemetery on your way home several times." He drove carefully, expertly. The truck's large tires ground through the deep snow until they were on the main street. He turned left, then left again. Just as they got to Fourteenth Street where she lived, Louise saw a car at the corner. In it sat her husband, and his face was lined with worry.

He must be hunting for me, Louise thought guiltily. *Oh, he's going to be angry. I was so foolish.* "Just let me out here," she told her driver. "That's my husband in that car. He's really going to yell at me. He told me not to go out to get my check."

The man didn't answer, but the strangest look crossed his face. Almost a look of sorrow, at least that's what Louise felt it was. He turned the truck and drove slowly down the street, stopping in front of her house.

She opened the door and got out, thanking him for helping her. She closed the door, and the truck drove slowly on. With trembling hands Louise let herself into the house. It was 4:15. She'd been in the blizzard for three hours.

Her first thought was to get warm, so she heated some water and fixed a hot drink. She couldn't get the young man out of her mind. He'd spoken so gently to her. He'd told her that she was almost frozen; that she could have frozen to death. *Could that be true?* she wondered. *Three hours. I was out there three hours! What if he hadn't seen me and come by?*

She dreaded Al coming in. He was going to be so upset. Eventually the door opened and he stepped inside, but he didn't say a word.

Louise told him that she'd seen him when she'd passed in the pickup, but he said that he'd sat at the corner for a long time—looking for her—and no truck had passed him. No car, no truck, no nothing. The weather was too bad. No one was out.

She didn't reply. The whole experience seemed strange. Almost unreal. She sat down near the heater, thinking through the experience.

"I know where you live," the man had told her. "I've seen you a lot of times." *But if he worked up at the shed, he wouldn't see me,* she reasoned. *The cemetery's too big.*

You can't see across it.

"My boss told me to come get you."

His boss?

Suddenly Louise gasped. In her mind she saw the young man; his clear eyes and kind face; his look of sorrow as they'd passed her angry, worried husband. She remembered that he knew the way home, knew which was her house.

A deep sense of awe filled her soul. "Thank You, Father," she breathed. "I don't know why You did it. I don't know why You chose me. But I will remember this for the rest of my life."

God has hosts of angels ministering to those who are "heirs of salvation."

Jehovah Sabbaoth, Lord of hosts.

It's one of His names.

PROMISE

"For He shall give His angels charge over you, to keep you in all your ways" (Ps. 91:11, NKJV).

Chapter 16

HE HEALS
THE BROKENHEARTED

Twenty-six-year-old Shannon Bigger had been excited when she landed a one-year internship with the Washington Adventist Hospital Foundation. Moving from her home in Washington State, she took an apartment in Takoma Park, Maryland. She was careful to find a place with good security, and not far from her work.

Now her year was almost over, and it had been a good year. In two short weeks she'd be moving back out west. She'd join the staff at Gem State Academy in Caldwell, Idaho. She was happy that she'd be closer to her family, and they were eager to have her settled in her first "real job," doing what she loved.

She was a dainty, caring, and vivacious young woman, and it was her nature to be sensitive to the needs of others. She made new friends at the Silver Spring Seventh-day Adventist Church and was soon a part of everything going on there. She'd spent a year as a student missionary on the island of Yap, teaching the first graders. Now in Silver Spring she was again involved in a life of ministry.

She'd thrown herself into her internship with the same

energy and enthusiasm that marked everything she did. On that tragic Father's Day she spent some time with her cousins, and then went back to her apartment. Later that evening one of her cousins phoned her but got no response. He called several times that evening, and grew a little concerned when she didn't answer. The next morning he phoned her office and discovered that she hadn't come in. So he went by her apartment, and was surprised to find her car still there in its parking space.

Now more than a little anxious, he rushed to Shannon's apartment. When she didn't answer the doorbell he tried the door. It was unlocked. What he found as he ran through the living area into her bedroom will forever be etched in his mind. Shannon was dead, the victim of a brutal attempted rape and murder.

He called the police, who came immediately, and the search for the criminal began. They discovered that Shannon's computer and other electronic equipment were missing. A closed-circuit camera in the parking lot had recorded the theft, so the police knew they were looking for a white van. They even had its license number. Less than 40 hours later the criminal, Anthony Robinson, was arrested.

Shannon died on June 16, 1996. It was both Father's Day and her grandfather's birthday.

The nightmare for the Bigger family began early Monday morning when the chaplain at Walla Walla College asked Shannon's parents, Darold and Barbara Bigger, to see him in his office. He sounded as though it was urgent. Barbara came from her work at the college store and tried to visit with the chaplain before Darold arrived, but for some reason she couldn't understand the pastor's mind wasn't on her conversation.

BECAUSE YOU PRAYED

Darold assumed that the chaplain wanted to see him about one of his students until he saw his wife there too. Then quietly closing the door, Pastor Knott looked at the couple. "I have the worst possible news I could ever share with you," he told them. "Shannon has been killed. Murdered in her apartment." In shocked unbelief, these two parents tried to process what they had just heard. *This can't be true.*

Barbara's first thought was *I must go to her*. And then she realized that it was too late. There was nothing she could do. In utter helplessness and grief, the day passed in a blur of phone calls, doorbells, friends' visits, contacts with other family members, sobbing, decisions, questions, sobbing . . . sobbing.

They decided to bring Shannon home for the funeral and burial, and Darold Bigger, professor of religion and social work at Walla Walla College, threw himself into planning the service. He was obsessive. Compulsive. Trying to manage every detail somehow became a mechanism for coping with his grief.

Each began the grieving process in their own way. Father, mother, sister, grandparents, aunts, uncles, cousins, and friends, each one trying to say goodbye to this special person who'd been snatched from them at such a young age. She had so much to live for, so much life ahead of her.

A big part of the healing process, both Darold and Barbara would later say, was the support and love that flooded over them from their family and friends. Prayers ascended around the clock for comfort and healing for this broken family and their broken hearts.

John Brunt, a colleague of many years, came to their

home as soon as he heard the terrible news, and "took over." He answered the phone and the doorbell, responding to a community reeling from shock, and stepped into the gap in his own bighearted way with love and unselfishness, sympathy, and understanding. God was using him. He was part of the healing.

Alden Thompson, a fellow professor, stopped by to share a quotation that again a loving God used for their inner solace and healing.

Doug Clark, another colleague and close family friend, was away on an archaeological dig in the Holy Land when he received the shocking news. He spent that next Sabbath climbing Mount Nebo and spent the day on top of the mountain, looking into the Promised Land. Alone on Mount Nebo he upheld the Bigger family to God, claiming promises on their behalf for healing.

"I have always dreaded what I would do if someone ever hurt my girls," Darold says. "I'm a man of ample temper and dogged determination; I've hoped strong friends would surround me at such a time to prevent me from doing something I would long regret.

"But those feelings didn't come. There was no teeth-clenching rage at Anthony, Shannon's killer; no seething passion for revenge. This wasn't my choice. It was a gift. I was surprised by grace. God's grace let me ignore Shannon's attacker and helped me to focus my anger on the real source of the problem, not just an example of it.

"Months later I had to face the anger and hatred, but initially God relieved me of that burden. What a wonderful gift from a gracious God."

God was answering the prayers of His children to do

His supernatural work on human hearts.

In due time the case came to trial. The young man pleaded guilty to attempted rape and brutal murder. His sentence: consecutive sentences of 20 years each, and life in prison without parole. Anthony sat stoic and emotionless as the judge pronounced his sentence. "This young man will suffer his own private hell, which he so richly deserves," the state's attorney said.

But revenge and hatred do not bring comfort. When the reporters questioned Darold and Barbara Bigger after the verdict and sentence they found that these two grieving parents showed no bitterness or desire for revenge. "Two families have lost children in this horrible experience," Darold said. "I'm sure it must be a terrible tragedy to see your son sentenced to prison for life for a senseless murder."

Shannon's mother was thankful to have the case closed. She said, "I looked for signs of repentance, of the realization of the gravity of what he had done. He didn't seem sorry. Maybe he isn't capable of that at this point."

It hadn't been easy for the Biggers to face Shannon's killer. And he was unrepentant; showing no sorrow or regret. In fact, he appealed his guilty plea and requested that his sentence be reduced!

When Darold was asked how he could be so at peace after suffering an irreparable loss, he told a news reporter, "This attitude isn't something that I have planned or orchestrated. It's a gift of God's amazing grace. This is not just a crime against Shannon, or her family and friends. It is another evidence of a terrible evil in this world that is going to take a Greater Power to change. We can pray for that."

As one news commentator concluded her report that

evening she said, "The verdict came on Good Friday, a time of forgiveness and redemption."

Truly, in all things God still works for the good of those who love Him (Rom. 8:28).

God can use parents' broken hearts, He can use a broken family to get the attention of thousands. The message echoes down from Calvary and the empty tomb—there is grace, there is hope, there is healing. This amazing grace is available to all those who will receive it. It enabled Darold and Barbara Bigger to forgive through their heartache. To claim the promise of the resurrection, when they'll be united with their joyful daughter.

The Biggers share their story—of loss, and of God's healing and faithfulness—and often Darold concludes by singing a song that meant so much to Shannon. This is a message of hope and a gift from him, as he sings in a clear tenor voice:

> "'Tis so sweet to trust in Jesus, just to take Him at
>   His word;
> Just to rest upon His promise, just to know, 'Thus
>   saith the Lord.'
> Jesus, Jesus, how I trust Him; how I've proved
>   Him o'er and o'er!
> Jesus, Jesus, precious Jesus! O for grace to trust
>   Him more!"

> "I'm so glad I learned to trust Thee, precious
>   Jesus, Savior, Friend.
> And I know that Thou art with me, wilt be with
>   me till the end.

Jesus, Jesus, how I trust Him; how I've proved it
o'er and o'er!

Jesus, Jesus, precious Jesus! O for grace to trust
Him more!"

Time is passing, and with its passing comes change. After some months the Biggers realized that there was less pain. They got through the first Christmas without her, the first anniversary of her death, and other special days in her life. Slowly they began to regain their own zest for life. God was continually granting healing, because "He heals the brokenhearted and binds up their wounds" (Ps. 147:3, NIV).

Sometime later, reading a list of Christ's attributes in Isaiah 9, Darold was prompted to pen these reasons to hope:

Why despair at depression when we know the Wonderful Counselor?

Why despair at the power of Satan when we know the Mighty God?

Why despair at the shortness of life when we know the Everlasting Father?

Why despair at evil when we know the Prince of Peace?

Why despair at suffering when we know the Divine Healer?

Why despair at failure when we know the Redeemer?

Why despair at death when we know the Creator of life?

God is faithful. He takes broken people, broken lives, and brings His healing.

He is *Jehoval Roha.* The Lord who heals.

It's one of His names.

Promises

"He heals the brokenhearted and binds up their wounds" (Ps. 147:3, NIV).

"For the Lord himself will come down from heaven . . . with the trumpet call of God, and the dead in Christ will rise first" (1 Thess. 4:16, NIV).

Chapter 17

I RESIGN!

You know her as the wife of Bob Dole, former speaker of the House.

You know that she served as a member of President Reagan's Cabinet and as president of the American Red Cross.

You know that she is respected as a woman of depth, warmth, and intelligence.

But you may not be aware that at one time she faced starvation. Spiritual starvation, when her high-pressure life and career crowded God to the edge of her priorities.

This is her story of how she welcomed Him back.

Elizabeth Dole. Child of God.

I had the privilege of hearing Elizabeth Dole speak in the Russell Senate Office Building at the United States National Day of Prayer. It was a day to face challenges, a day for those of us present to examine ourselves, to pray for our nation, for our leaders, and for one another. It was a spiritual feast day, and Elizabeth Dole's message tugged at my heart and inspired my soul. This is the story she told:

My spiritual journal began many years ago in a Carolina home where the gospel was as much a part of our lives as fried chicken and azaleas in the spring. Mom Cathey, my grandmother who lived to within two weeks of her 100th birthday, was my role model.

I and other neighborhood children spent many Sunday afternoons in her home drinking lemonade, eating cookies, and playing Bible games or listening to Mom Cathey read to us from her Bible. I have that Bible now, and it is one of my most cherished possessions.

She totally practiced what she preached and lived her life for others. In a tragic accident Mom Cathey lost a son at the hands of a drunk driver. The insurance policy on his life built a hospital wing in a far-off church mission in Pakistan. And although Mom was not wealthy, almost anything she could spare went to ministers at home and missions abroad. And when, in her 90s, she had to move to a nursing home, she welcomed the opportunity.

"Elizabeth," she told me (I can still hear her voice), "there might be some people there who don't know the Lord, and I can read the Bible to them."

In all the years I knew her I can't remember an unkind word escaping her lips or an ungracious deed marring her path. She was an almost perfect role model, and I wanted to be just like her.

And I had a good start. From an early age I had an active church life. But as we move along in life, how often in our busy lives something becomes a barrier to total commitment to God. In my case it was my career.

You know, these things can creep up on you without your even being aware of it. I was doing good things, working hard to excel, to achieve. I was competing against myself, not others. I wanted to do my *best*. There's nothing wrong with that. But I'm inclined to be a perfectionist, and it's very hard, you know, to control everything. It's hard to surmount every difficulty, to foresee every problem, to realize every opportunity.

And not only is such a goal tough on you; it can be very tough on your family and friends, and your fellow workers. In my case, my compulsion to achieve—to be perfect—began crowding out what Mom Cathey had taught me were life's most important priorities.

I was blessed with a beautiful marriage and a challenging career I loved. And yet, only gradually, over many years, did I realize something vital was missing—my life was threatened with spiritual starvation.

In my quest to be efficient, to do everything just right, I had filed God away somewhere between gardening and government. He was there, but only as one of many "to-do's." He was not a priority.

Realizing this, I began to pray about it. And leading me no faster than I was ready to go, God led me to people and circumstances that made a real difference in my life.

I found a tremendously sensitive, caring pastor who helped me see what joy there can be when God is the center of one's life and all else flows from that center.

I made time in my life to attend a Monday night prayer and fellowship meeting. Talking with others who shared my need to stretch and grow spiritually, I was strengthened myself. I joined Bible studies with other Senate wives and learned that one day a week can be set aside for spiritual and personal rejuvenation without the rest of the week falling apart.

I finally realized that if I try to save my life, I will lose it all. I felt God calling me to total commitment, to literally lay my life on the line for Him.

"If anyone would come after me," Jesus tells us, "he must deny himself and take up his cross and follow me. For whoever wants to save his life will lose it, but whoever loses his life for me will find it. What good will it be for a man if he gains the whole world, yet forfeits his soul?" (Matt. 16:24-26, NIV).

These were hard words to swallow when I was doing my own thing, but the most compelling logic I'd ever heard. For if Christ is who He says He is—our Saviour, the one who gives meaning to a world of confusing, conflicting priorities—I had to realize that I could not compartmentalize Christ. I had to let Him be the center of my life.

It was time to stop living my life backwards, time to put Christ first, to put Him in the very center of my life. It was time to submit my resignation as sovereign of my own little universe.

God accepted my resignation.

And God taught me that it is not what I do that matters, but what a sovereign God chooses to do through me. God doesn't want worldly success. He wants my heart, in submission to Him. Life is not just a few years to spend on self-indulgence and career advancement. Life is a privilege and a responsibility, a stewardship to a much higher calling. God's calling. This alone gives true meaning to life.

The biblical story of Esther grew to be a powerful lesson to me. When Queen Esther told Mordecai that the king had signed a decree that would kill all the Jews, Mordecai told her that she had to go to the king and inform him of this atrocious deed. "And who knows, but that you have come . . . for such a time as this?" (Esther 4:14, NIV).

That spoke to me. I realized that each of us—and that included me—has a God-given assignment in this world. We are to love and serve those within our own sphere of influence. No one can do it for us.

We have been blessed to be a blessing; we've received that we might give.

I needed to hear this challenge. I need to continually hear it—this call to be yielded to Him.

Esther called for prayer and fasting, and then she cast her very life upon God in dependence on Him.

So often I've found myself faced with tasks that demand wisdom and courage far beyond my own. And not just in the big decisions. I am constantly in need of God's grace to preform life's routine duties with the love for others, the peace and joy inherent in God's call.

And I, an independent woman, have learned that dependence is a good thing. That when I've used up my own resources, when I can't make things come out my way, when I'm willing to trust God with the outcome, when I'm weak—then I am strong. Only then am I in the best position to feel Christ's power rest upon me. Feel it encourage me, replenishing my energy and deepening my faith.

Yielding your life to Christ is a high and difficult calling. I'll struggle with it for the rest of my life. But I know that for me it's the only life worth living, the only life worthy of my Lord.

The world is ripe and ready for men and women who

recognize they are not immune from the predicaments of the day, men and women who are willing to accept the privilege of serving and who are ready to see that the providence of God may have brought them into the world "for such a time as this."

By God's grace, I will be one of them.

For God is not only our Saviour, He also wants to be our Lord, and there's a difference. He wants us to choose Him daily as Lord and Master, and give Him control.

Jesus Christ, Lord.

It's one of His names.

PROMISES

I realized that if I tried to save my life, I would lose it.

"As the heavens are higher than the earth, so are my ways higher than your ways and my thoughts than your thoughts" (Isa. 55:9, NIV).

Chapter 18

A NICKEL
A CHICKEN

God often surprises us. Have you noticed? He loves to gently amaze us with His infinite ability to help us, to rescue us, to provide, to give victory. The strong and encouraging message of Psalm 50:15 is "I want you to trust me in your times of trouble, so I can rescue you, and you can give me glory" (TLB).

No two of our stories are the same, but here is one that illustrates that the God of the universe is still willing and able to give us just the help we need. He is indeed the God who gives us victory.

Harland Sanders was 6 years old when his father died. With three children to care for, his mother had to find work. So she did, first operating a sewing machine in a garment factory, then sorting vegetables in a cannery. Being the oldest, Harland was left each day as the family baby-sitter. And the family cook.

Mother Sanders knew that her children were going to need more help with their growing up than she would be able to give them, so she faithfully took them to church.

Harland was impressed. He loved the stories. He loved the music. He loved to hear about Jesus' love for him. Often he found himself retelling the stories to his brother and sister in his role as weekday guardian.

As he approached his teens, however, church interested him less and less. He learned to be resourceful and clever, and decided that he could depend on his own skill and ingenuity to get what he wanted, rather than depending on God.

Harland worked hard. He became an effective salesman—tires, insurance, gasoline. He married and settled in the little town of Corbin, Kentucky, where he opened a service station. With his penchant for cooking it was not uncommon to see him after hours bent over the little stove in the humble room behind the gas station where he lived. Now and then he'd invite travelers who stopped to buy gas to also sample his cooking. Each agreed this was home cooking at its best.

Before long word began to spread through central Kentucky that you could get some mighty good food at Sanders' place. He put some chairs in the corner of the gas station and eventually was selling more food than gas. To accommodate the new clientele he tore down the gas station and built a restaurant that seated 142 customers, and a motel.

He was doing what he liked, making good money and lots of friends. By the time he was 35 his restaurant had been featured in Duncan Hines' *Adventures in Good Eating* as a place where some of the country's best food could be found. Including Southern fried chicken.

But then his fortunes changed. The Federal Highway Department rerouted the highway, and Sanders found himself sitting on a lonely road with a large restaurant and a large debt. He did the only thing he could do. He sold the business to pay his debts.

Broke and broken now, Harland did what he had not done for a long time—he looked up. His early religious training caused him to see the hand of God in these setbacks, and he sensed that God was working through them to get his attention. Harland went back to church. He also began to pray—for wisdom, for guidance, and for another chance to succeed so he could somehow give God the glory.

He promised God that if He would help him, that he would "give God His share." Harland never forgot that promise. He was able to give enormous amounts to charities and educational projects.

Armed with his newly rekindled faith, a Social Security check for $105, and a good dose of Southern-bred determination, Sanders set out to seek a new direction in his life. His one asset: a proven recipe for fried chicken.

So it was that one overcast day he climbed into his old Ford and started down the highway with a recipe and an idea. At the first likely-looking restaurant he approached the owner and asked a disarming favor. "Let me cook some fried chicken for your customers during the noon hour. If they like it, I'll sell you the recipe." The experiment was a success. So was it at the next restaurant, and the next.

Sleeping in his car with a pressure cooker, flour, and seasonings, Sanders went from town to town offering his secret to interested restaurant owners. And his franchise arrangement just may be the simplest and most effective in all franchise history. "Send me a nickel for every chicken you sell," he'd tell them. They'd shake hands on it, and Sanders would be off to another town, another restaurant.

"I don't think I lost a nickel with my handshake agreement," Sanders said. In two years' time he had $1,000 a day rolling in, and franchises were selling as fast as fried chicken from coast to coast. In 1964, at the age of 75, Sanders sold Kentucky Fried Chicken for $364,000,000, staying on as technical advisor and "ambassador of goodwill."

My mother and I visited with the colonel and his wife, Claudia, in their home where he told me his story. They lived in a comfortable but modest two-story, 10-room house east of Louisville, Kentucky. We felt welcomed by their warmth and charm. And we laughed often as this unique man told candidly of his foibles and blunders. But frequently his testimony resounded with the lesson he had learned: "You can't do anything without God."

I invited him to visit both Kettering Medical Center, where I was working at the time, and nearby Spring Valley Academy, since I knew he loved young people. He and his driver spent the day with us, and what a day it was! He obviously enjoyed every part of it—except the food. Not that it wasn't well prepared and delicious; it was just different from his usual diet.

"Ruthie," he confided to me with a smile playing at the corners of his mouth, "there's a good oyster place in Cincinnati, and I think we're going to stop there on our way home." We laughed together, and he knew I wasn't offended. He was a delightful guest.

He especially enjoyed visiting the school. "Aren't kids the finest folk in the world!" he'd say. We offered him a guided tour, but he had his own ideas. Walking down the hall, he'd suddenly open a classroom door unannounced and step inside.

He was immediately recognizable. At six feet tall and 200 pounds, he was an imposing figure. Add the snow-white hair, white mustache, white goatee, white suit, white shirt set off by a black string tie, and black shoes, and he was unmistakable. The outfit was his trademark and appropriate for a Kentucky colonel. (The title was an honorary one, conferred by the governor of Kentucky when Sanders was in his early 30s.)

Colonel Harland Sanders achieved wealth, fame, and great respect from his fellow citizens. His company grew from a one-man business operating out of the trunk of an old Ford into one of the giants in the food industry. But he loved to tell that the thing that brought him some of his greatest joy was a personal victory.

For many years Sanders had struggled with what he called his "emphatic language" (his euphemism for swearing). Only one person ever said anything to him about it, but what he said stopped him in his tracks.

"Colonel, I want to say something to you," a man in Richmond, Virginia, confronted him one warm summer afternoon. "Nobody can appreciate all the cussin' you do."

Startled by the man's frankness, "I apologized right then," the colonel told us. But he immediately sensed that apologizing wasn't enough. "I knew it was a vicious habit that diluted my witness as a Christian, and I knew that I had to do something about it. But I had tried to quit before, without success.

"This time I took it to the Lord," the colonel told me. "I asked Him to clean up my mouth, to make my words clean and wholesome. To change my heart so I didn't even think those words. And He did it. He did it! He rescued me from myself and from a habit I was helpless to conquer." It was a precious victory.

Colonel Sanders learned that God truly is *Jehovah Nissi*—the Lord who is my banner of victory.

It's one of His names.

PROMISE

"I want you to trust me in your times of trouble, so I can rescue you, and you can give me glory" (Ps. 50:15, TLB).

Chapter 19

ORPHANS
WITH A FATHER

I can never forget the first time my husband and I drove up in front of Mueller's orphanage in Bristol, England. It's not an orphanage now, for England's underprivileged children no longer roam the streets. But the five huge stone buildings—now part of a technical college—still stand after a century, and are a dramatic tribute to the strength of one man's faith and the power of that man's God.

George Mueller's story has inspired me, as it has millions, ever since I first heard it. He had one all-consuming goal: to demonstrate that God answers prayer. He chose to display the picture of a faithful God by providing for orphans who at the time were roaming homeless on the streets of London and other of England's cities. He decided that he would do so totally as an act of faith, never asking anyone for anything. Starting with only a few children, there were times when more than 5,000 were in his care. But let me begin at the beginning.

George's friends were surprised when he enrolled in the theology course at Halle Divinity School. He was known for his carousing, dishonesty, and hard drinking rather than for his piety. He and his friends loved to travel about Europe staying in the finest hotels, eating at the finest eateries, then sneaking off to the next city without paying their bills. On occasion when he was discovered and caught, his father, after paying the bill, would attempt to pound a sense of right and wrong into young George with severe beatings. But it seemed that nothing could change George Mueller's heart.

That is, until one spring evening. He and a former drinking buddy accepted an invitation to the home of a friend where a prayer meeting was to be held. They had seen it as a purely social occasion, but God had other plans. George found a small group of earnest believers kneeling in prayer, talking to a God whom they knew was listening. They opened the Bible and read its words as though it were God Himself speaking to them.

George found something happening in the group he didn't understand. But he found himself drawn irresistibly to it. Slowly the God of the prodigal son was calling another prodigal to Himself. Mueller would never be the same. He began to search for ways to tell the story of the all-sufficient God he had met in a humble house on Barnaby Street.

Mueller married Mary Groves, a woman of strong faith, whose brother was caring for orphans in eastern Europe. Mueller was fascinated by his brother-in-law's faith since the small orphanage had no visible means of support. God was the sufficient supplier. George pondered whether he might begin a similar ministry in England by which not only could hundreds of children be helped, but through which the all-sufficient power of God could be displayed.

Pastoring in southern England was something of a test of faith in itself for the young couple. It was common practice to pay the pastor's salary by "renting the pews" of the church. Each family would pay monthly for a place to sit when they came to church.

One crisp autumn morning Pastor Mueller explained to his congregation that he was changing the process by which his support would be provided. Instead of renting their pews, there would be a box at the back of the church and the people were simply invited to give offerings for the pastor as the Lord impressed them. It was an act of faith for George and his young wife, but one that would prepare them for the greater tests that would come.

Mueller could not erase from his mind the plight of the children of London, thousands orphaned when their parents died of the plagues that ravaged the country. Countless of them were malnourished, sleeping in alleys, eating from garbage cans, stealing to survive. Finally Pastor Mueller and his wife became convinced that God was calling them to leave the relative comfort of a traditional pastorate and come to the rescue of the orphans on London streets.

George and Mary's prayers became increasingly specific. They prayed for a house, for food, for furniture, for clothing, for everything they would need to open a home for orphans. Mueller had made the decision that he would never ask for funds, because as he liked to say, his "Banker in heaven had more than enough resources."

God provided a home on Wilson Street. He also provided food, furniture, clothing, and staff. Everything they needed. Monday morning Mueller and his fledgling staff arrived at the new house ready to welcome the homeless children who would be drawn there by the promise of a clean bed, ample food, and warm love. But none came.

It was a quiet, thoughtful Mueller as he and Mary walked home that evening and discussed the disappointments of the day. George was serious; Mary was amused. "George," she told him, "you prayed for everything, and the Lord provided as you knew He would. But you neglected to ask Him to send children." That night they knelt together and prayed for God to send needy children to the orphans' home. The next day the children came.

Throughout his lifetime Mueller received millions of unsolicited dollars—to build the new buildings and feed and clothe the orphans. That story is well known. What is not so well known is that he also gave away large sums to support Christian schools, publishing work, missionaries, and scores of other worthwhile projects. For instance, Hudson Taylor's highly effective work in China was made possible because of Mueller's faithful donations to the China Inland Mission.

As the story of Mueller's orphanages spread he was approached by would-be donors asking about his needs. His answer was always the same. He would tell them that he only discussed these matters with his Banker in heaven. Even when there was no money for the next meal, his answer was always the same. At least twice through these years Mueller called the children to the dinner table though there was no food in the cupboard. On both occasions, even as Mueller was thanking God for providing for their needs, there was a knock at the door, and an unknown benefactor stood there with food for that meal and more.

George Mueller's life remains an exhibit to the faithfulness of God. Here was a humble Christian who determined that his life would testify to God's ability to meet our every need. He stands as a spiritual giant who hung on in spite of epidemics, financial predicaments, and daunting circumstances. God gave this rebellious youth a genuine transformation and a never-say-die faith. In his journal, Mueller recorded 50,000 answers to prayer.

For 10 years or more I had been asking God for my own "Mueller experience." I wanted a small taste of what he had. I wanted my life also to attest to the fact that our heavenly Father is imminently trustworthy. My work presented constant opportunities for me to ask Him for special favors.

A seminar was announced for the Portland, Oregon, area where my husband and I were living, and it occurred to me that many of our pastors might be blessed by attending. But that would cost money. Without telling anyone, I began praying for $10,000 to subsidize their travel and registration costs.

One morning, a few days before the deadline, a physician walked into my office and asked if I needed some money. I told him I had been praying about it, and he replied that he had just left a check with the conference treasurer for me to use as needed. The check was for $10,000.

That remarkable answer to prayer prompted me to ask God for more, and over the next several years, before we left the West Coast, God provided more than $300,000 for just such projects. Most of this was provided when God was the only one who knew about the need.

When my husband and I moved to Maryland and joined the staff of the North American Division, I was asked to direct the work of Prayer Ministries for the North American church. However, funding was needed to cover the costs. So I prayed, daily asking the Lord for financial help.

As we were leaving the West Coast for Maryland a friend told us that he saw God's hand in the way his business was prospering. He said that he believed the Lord was leading him to support various needs in the church. I remember well his words: "When you get to Maryland, if you have needs for funding projects, I hope you'll remember me. I'd like to help."

So, because he had offered, I contacted him, and he supported Prayer Ministries generously for three years. I contacted several other friends who had indicated their interest in giving to this work also, but I became more and more convinced I wasn't following God's leading in my life. I had been asking God for a George Mueller experience, and Mueller would never have told others of his financial needs.

I understand that many people have no qualms about asking others for money. And there are many who have the capacity to give who like to know when there are specific needs. And there is biblical precedent. Nehemiah, for instance, was led to inform the king of his needs, and God impressed the king to give in response. I don't wish to minimize the legitimacy of that means of financing kingdom projects. But because I had been praying for a specific faith practice such as Mueller had followed, I became less comfortable, even about calling my donor to let him know I needed his help. (He had committed a certain amount annually, and I would remind him each year when it needed to be sent.)

The conviction grew so unmistakably in my heart that one day I phoned him. "I'm sorry that I've asked each year for your help," I said. "From now on I will only pray about my needs. If He impresses you to send the funds as you have been, that will be fine. If not, I will know He wants you to provide help for some other ministry instead."

I talked to the other donors also, explaining that I would no longer be contacting them for funds. I told them I earnestly longed to give God opportunity to demonstrate His faithfulness without my having to ask anyone but Him. One of my friends objected. She felt this "new approach" would put Prayer Ministries at risk, and she told me so. But as we talked it through and prayed about it, we both had peace.

So 1998 Prayer Ministries began with only the funds available from the North American Division, about one third of the total budget. Daily I lifted the ministry before the Lord, asking Him to provide. In March our treasurer, George Crumley, contacted me and said, "Ruthie, I think it's time for you to contact your donor; your funds are nearly depleted."

I explained that this year I wasn't going to ask for money, that I would pray for funding and wait for God to provide according to His riches. "If the Lord chooses not to provide, I'll know He has other plans," I assured Elder Crumley. "In Isaiah 54 He reminds us that we will not be ashamed or disgraced, and I believe He wants to fulfill that promise today as He did in Isaiah's day."

As time passed my prayers took on a new intensity. At first I had just claimed Bible promises that God would provide for our needs. But studying the stories of how He had met the needs of His children throughout Scripture gave me the courage to become very specific.

By mid-April our funds were nearly exhausted. I was at Dulles Airport en route to Andrews University when I ran into Elder Crumley. He told me the situation was dire. "Just let me know when to stop," I told him. I was ready to do that—to stop this ministry and wait for God's timing to begin it again, or for Him to call someone else to its leadership.

My prayers had changed. Instead of praying for God to provide, I asked that I might know His will. God made me willing to submit to His will, and all through April I felt the peace of His presence.

I often kept a list of Bible promises with me and when I was alone I would personalize them and claim them for my needs. In the car one day, I had a sheet of paper on the seat beside me and at each stop light I'd glance down at the paper and note a new text to give direction to my praying.

A little song began to form in my mind, combining two of the promises about which I'd been praying. "I can do all things through Christ who strengthens me" (Phil. 4:13, NKJV) and "I want you to trust me in your times of trouble, so I can rescue you, and you can give me glory" (Ps. 50:15, TLB). I put these promises together and from a grateful heart began to sing:

We can do all things, you can do all things,
I can do all things because He loves me.
We can do all things, you can do all things,
I can do all things in Jesus' name.

He gives me the courage, He provides the strength.
He has great resources, He'll go to any length
To reach His ones in trouble. He's promised to be there,
He'll rescue you because you're in the center
of His care.

In the past I had called my donor to pray with him. He was carrying enormous loads on his shoulders, including responsibility for his hundreds of employees and their families. I had not phoned him since January because I didn't want it to be interpreted as an indirect reminder that it was time for him to send the check. But I care a great deal about this family, and I didn't want to cut him and his wife out of my life.

Before picking up the phone I prayed, "Lord, it's OK if I never get another dollar from him. I don't want money to come between him and me; I don't want to compromise my desire to live by faith. Keep Your hand over this phone conversation so I'll have opportunity to pastor him but it will not be seen as a request for money."

I called his office, but because of schedule complications it was about a week before we made contact by phone. We had a wonderful visit and I had opportunity to pray for him, for his wife, and for their family. He told me some of the providential happenings on a recent trip, and we thanked God together. Neither of us mentioned money, and I was relieved.

A few weeks later my husband and I were riding home from the office together. We were discussing the day's events when he handed me an envelope. I recognized the stationery; it was from my donor. My hands trembled as I opened it. Inside was a check for $100,000.

I phoned him as soon as we arrived home. I had to know if he'd written the check after my call. He was busy when I finally got through to his home, so I talked to his wife, explaining that if he had sent the check because of my call I would have to send it back. Later when I spoke to him he told me he had sent the check two days before I had called to pray.

"I appreciate it so much," I told him—a huge understatement—"but I didn't ask you for money." He laughed, "I know you didn't. But Someone else did!"

"I know who that is," I said, "I talk to Him about you every day." We enjoyed that together, and praised the Lord.

I hung up and phoned Elder Crumley. "Hello, this is Ruthie," I said.

He sounded disappointed to get my call. I didn't know why, until he said, "Did you get my e-mail today?"

"No, I haven't checked my e-mail yet," I told him.

"Well," he continued solemnly, "I sent you a notice that today is the last day. The funds are exhausted. You have reached the end of your budget."

We rejoiced together as I told him of the check. "Ruthie," he said, "that money is from the Lord."

"God has a heaven full of blessings," says Ellen White in *Christ's Object Lessons*, for those who will ask in faith. In the same chapter is a powerful sentence that reminds us God longs for us to ask Him for great things.

A promise I often quote to Him in prayer shows His lavish way of dealing with us. "The Lord will open to you His good treasure . . . and to bless all the work of your hand. You shall lend to many nations, but you shall not borrow" (Deut. 28:12, NKJV).

George Mueller saw God fulfill that promise in his life. Mueller was able to be a channel of God's "good treasure" to people all over the world. From these promises another song came to me:

> You said You would open heaven's door
> > Where Your abundant blessings wait in store.
> You have so great a plan, to bless the work of
> > Your child's hands.
> You said You would open heaven's door.

You said You would open Your good treasure.
  You even said that it would bring You pleasure
To have Your children ask, for You it's not a task;
  You said You would give it without measure.

You're the one who opens heaven's door.
  You've promised You would bless us more
    and more.
Jehovah God, You're here; You even tell us not
    to fear.
  You're the one who opens heaven's door.

Through my "Mueller experience" I learned that God often gives tangible answers to prayer so we will have faith to ask Him for the really big things. What are the really big things? Acceptance of His love; assurance of salvation; faith; confidence to reach out to others in need. And let me hasten to assure you that if He'll answer my prayers, He'll answer anybody's. It's not my faith; it's His faithfulness.

God wants us to know that He still provides.

He is *Jehovah Jireh.* The Lord who provides.

It's one of His names.

PROMISES

"The one who calls you is faithful" (1 Thess. 5:24, NIV).

"It's not my faith. It's His faithfulness" (George Mueller).

CHOICES, CHOICES

W hen I came here, I was mad at God," Teresa began. "I thought I hated Him. I really didn't understand much about Him, and I just couldn't put things together in my life."

Teresa was one of four teenagers from Hawaii who attended the North American Teen Prayer and Ministry Conference at Southwestern Adventist University in September 1997. During the closing service, as many of the kids were reflecting on their experiences and praising God for what He'd done that weekend, Teresa walked up to the platform and with a smile looked across the church. It had been a long journey from Hawaii. But it couldn't compare to the journey she had made that weekend back to God. She had gone from darkness to light.

Growing up in a broken home, Teresa had developed into a troubled teenager. She'd hardly known why she'd been chosen to attend the prayer conference or why she'd agreed to go. And she felt out of place with her pierced navel and bare midriff, uncomfortable with the stares and whispers of some of her peers.

"But as I've been here this weekend and watched Him working in the lives of other kids, it has slowly occurred to me that this is *real,*" she told the teenage congregation. "And I don't want to miss it! So I've asked God to do something special for me." She paused for a mere heartbeat. "I have never experienced this kind of Friend—and hope—before. I just want to thank God for meeting me here."

Where God met her was in the dormitory room she shared with two other girls who'd come from Hawaii. In that small room Teresa came face-to-face with deep issues in her life. She'd just been confronted with the love of Jesus in a powerful sermon by José Rojas, and wanted to commit herself to Christ. But something inside wouldn't let her.

"Auntie" Michelle Siebel and her friends prayed with Teresa and encouraged her to give her life to Jesus. Again and again came her reply: "I just can't." She felt abandoned by the important people in her life, and didn't think she could make such a big commitment alone. She felt sure that even if she did she'd never be able to follow through with it.

More prayers, more tears, more "I can'ts."

Finally Michelle said, "Teresa, you are afraid because you think that you'll be all alone, but it is really just the opposite. Jesus will be there. He will never leave you. No matter what, He is going to help you in your commitments. He made you. He understands."

As the magnitude of this eternal truth dawned, Teresa smiled through her tears. "Yes," she whispered. "If He will be there, I want Him."

Teresa and her friends have been busy in the year since that prayer conference, sharing their stories and praying with others. The lives of teens from all over Hawaii have been changed because they see God in Teresa and her friends.

These teens in Hawaii—and in other places—are finding that the revival that God brings is a deeply personal experience, and it leads to reformation. They are literally and willingly changed.

These young adults are looking at lifestyle issues. They're making decisions about music, television, movies, videos, jewelry, and which foods are best for their bodies. They're asking, "How is my life affected by what I put into my mouth, into my mind, into my heart?" They are making clothing choices from time spent on their knees rather than from time spent at the mall.

They want to know what God meant when He said to Joshua, "Purify yourselves, for tomorrow the Lord will do great wonders among you" (Joshua 3:5, NLT). They are asking God to do great wonders for them. And He is. He is providing light.

In one small Bible study group as together teens and young adults focused on the law of God, one commented, "I just don't think that this law, given so long ago, has much relevance in our lives today."

All eyes went to Chino as he began to speak. "Now wait a minute. I just got out of prison. I was there for breaking the law, and I can tell you that laws are important and necessary. God's laws are the most significant. I was in prison because I'd rebelled in my heart. I had turned completely from God. But in that terrible place I fell on my face before God and promised Him that even though it seemed totally impossible from a human standpoint, if He'd somehow get me out of there I would give Him everything.

"It's still hard to believe, but I'm free! God did it. And

I'm here to tell you that law is important."

Chino could hardly believe his own ears. He hadn't planned to be so vulnerable. He didn't want to tell his story, and vowed he would never do that again. But God had other plans, and wherever Chino tells his story hearts are broken and the power of the Holy Spirit changes the lives of those who hear him.

The number of teens involved in this ministry is growing, and they're serious about being Christians. They meet together regularly for prayer and Bible study, and then, empowered by the Holy Spirit, they go out to tell others what God has done and is doing for them. Occasionally, they pray for three hours or longer, greatly blessed as they "conversationally" talk to God as with a close friend. Sometimes they even sing their prayers.

This little group is growing and is blessing the entire state of Hawaii. On the island of Kauai the group of teens led out in evangelism.

One Saturday night as several teens were studying together, Chino and one of his friends brought out a handful of plastic compact disk holders and passed them around through the group. "We've just destroyed hundreds of dollars' worth of CDs," Chino told the group.

"Why?" someone asked.

"You're kidding!" another exclaimed, studying the CD titles and names of the performers. "You've thrown away a lot of our favorites."

"Yeah, but just look at these covers," Chino and his friend told them. "Have you really listened to the words on these songs? They're wrong. Their whole purpose is to destroy character."

The teens talked about this for a long time. Several began to realize that if they wouldn't *do* what the words of the songs suggested—if it were wrong to do those things—then why would Christians willingly put the lyrics in their minds over and over again? Thoughtfully, others were convicted that they needed to go through their own CDs.

And so the Holy Spirit continues His work in their lives, His work of shedding light.

God is truly doing the "new thing" that He has promised in Isaiah 43:19. He is using the youth, as He has pointed out in Joel 2:28. He purifies; He goes with us; it is He who teaches, cleanses, changes.

It's like the boy who gave Jesus his lunch, and the lunch fed 5,000 and more. The lad must have been wide-eyed all day, and then when someone said that Jesus wanted his lunch, he was curious and honored. His eyes never left the little basket because his own stomach was empty, but he was eager to see what Jesus would do with his food. With wonder and awe he watched Jesus break the bread and dried fishes, and finally when he was served, he too enjoyed the simple, nourishing food. And suddenly he realized that Christ had used his lunch to feed everyone.

I can just hear him excitedly trying to tell his mother his story, to explain how he felt on that incredible day. "You'll *never* believe what this kind Man did with my lunch," he says. Then as he thinks about the possibilities, he adds, "I wonder what He would do if I gave Him *everything.*"

And that is exactly what enables God to be effective in our lives—our obedience, our willingness to follow His light. There is a beautiful little chorus that says it like this:

"Walk in the light, beautiful light,
  walk where the dewdrops of mercy shine bright,
  Shine all around us—by day and by night,
  Jesus, the Light of the world."

He shines in us because He is the Light of the world.
It's one of His names.

PROMISES

"I am the Light of the world. If you follow me, you won't be stumbling through the darkness, because you will have the light that leads to life" (John 8:12, NLT).

The Light of Israel was to "burn and devour . . . thorns and briers." We can bring the useless branches, the unpleasant, unlovely things of life, into the light of His presence to be consumed.

"And the light of Israel shall be for a fire, and his Holy One for a flame: and it shall burn and devour his thorns and his briers in one day" (Isa. 10:17).

Chapter 21

DOES GOD KNOW ABOUT AIRPLANES FOR SALE?

G od sent us the plane, but we can't afford to fly it. What do you suppose He wants us to do now?" It was a sobering question, especially for the students involved in a gigantic faith venture. It appeared that up to this point God had opened every single door, but now the project seemed destined to collapse. You and I might ask the same question: "What to do now?"

David Gates and his family have given more than 18 years of service to their church, primarily in South America and the Caribbean. David is a nurse, a skilled pilot, and a computer whiz. But undergirding these skills he is a venturesome Christian who thrives on taking God at His word. "I love to give God opportunities to show that He is still powerful," David says with a smile. "And He is."

Now the setting: Guyana is a little splotch of earth on the northeast coast of South America, 500 miles from one end to the other. Its shores are washed by the warm waters of the tropical Atlantic. Three-quarters of a million people live in Guyana. It is the only English-speaking country in South America, and has one of the lowest gross national products of any. Life expectancy is 64; infant morality is high. Nearly 90 percent of the country is covered by dense tropical forests, and there are few paved roads. The country receives about 90 inches of rainfall each year.

David Gates and his family felt a call from God to help the people of this beautiful land—to help them with their health needs and to tell them the story of the gospel. He also knew that parts of this country could be reached only by air. But he had no airplane and no money to buy one or to maintain it. So they turned to the only source they knew of that has infinite resources: God. They were opening their mouths wide as God invites us to do in Psalm 81:10. He says, "Open your mouth wide and see if I won't fill it. You will receive every blessing you can use!" (TLB).

Two years earlier, and before this urgent prayer for a plane for Guyana, David and his family had prayed for a small airplane for work in the Caribbean. Within mere months of their specific prayers, God provided a plane, exactly what they needed to begin their work. Now, after two years, more and more requests for help were coming in, but David could meet only a small percentage of them. God was asking him to expand. It was time for another airplane—another miracle. This plane—for Guyana—would need to be larger.

Enter Don Starlinn, an instructor in the aviation program at Andrews University, and president of a volunteer group called Adventist World Aviation (AWA). David and Don worked closely together on the Board of this fledgling organization, so Don knew all about David's needs and prayers for Guyana.

Don says that "after hearing of David's concern for

Guyana, we began our fall quarter with a great sense of urgency. We believed that God wanted us not only to learn something so we could serve Him better, but to become something so He could use us for His plans. I had a class of would-be pilot-mechanic-missionaries, and they were serious about being available for God's assignments."

Don describes some of his aviation classes in these words: "As we spent time praying and in God's Word, we often found ourselves weeping in repentance and in longing for the will of God. The Holy Spirit became a sweet presence in our classroom. We came to believe that nothing is too hard for the Lord. I guess He wanted us to know that first."

But back to Guyana. You may not have priced airplanes lately, but they don't come cheap. Still, the class began to join David in his prayers for a plane for Guyana. The cost, they were told, of buying a twin-engine airplane required for the long trips over unbroken tropical jungles and getting it ready could be as much as $300,000!

So now the question: Does God know about airplanes for sale?

Dr. Ray Nelson, in Santa Cruz, California had decided to sell his plane—a twin engine NAVION. Here the plot thickens, because as he advertised and got ready to sell, two men became very interested in the plane. Each was ready to pay the asking price. The first buyer owned three restaurants, and was sure that this plane was exactly what he was looking for. He and Dr. Nelson discussed the sale. Everything was ready, but at the time of the "closing" they couldn't seem to make contact. Nelson couldn't understand it.

Later the second man was ready to buy the plane, but

at the last minute this sale also crumbled. There was no logical explanation! This got Dr. Nelson's attention! As he and his wife looked back in wonderment at the loss of two sure sales, the thought came to them: *Do you suppose God wants this plane?* They decided that He did, so they called Don Starlinn and the AWA office.

And it was settled. Dr. and Mrs. Nelson made a gift of the twin-engined plane—for Guyana! It was perfectly suited for the long-range, medical-evangelistic work in Guyana and the Caribbean.

In the final class Starlinn told his students about Dr. Nelson's gift. They fell on their knees to thank God for this miracle. As they rejoiced together at this incredible evidence of God's providence, one of the students had a thought. "You know, I can see why we had to wait for the plane," he said. "Experiencing and finding God is more important than a miracle, and getting the plane right away would have been a distraction. God wanted us to know Him first."

Much still had to be accomplished to get the plane ready for travel over jungles and water. Adventist World Aviation would hold the title to the plane and raise money for its support. Over several weeks the funds appeared, the work progressed, the test flights were completed, and the time for departure for Guyana approached.

Oh, yes. There was the question of insurance. It's expensive to insure an airplane. Especially a twin. Especially one that will be flying over miles of unbroken jungle with no airstrips. Especially an older one. It didn't seem a good risk to any of the aircraft insurance underwriters in the United States.

God was stretching their faith. "God, You have provided the plane, and now we need the insurance." Their requests were simple and sincere. More searching. They went to the same companies again, expecting that God would lead one of them to change and grant their request. Nothing. "God sent us the plane, but we can't fly it. What do you suppose He wants us to do now?"

Finally, a few days from departure time, a large international company in Europe agreed to insure the plane—for a $10,000 annual insurance premium! That was twice what they'd expected to pay and far beyond their reach. Again they lifted their hearts to God in prayer.

They could identify with the desperation of King Hezekiah when he faced his crisis of impossibilities. The king went to the temple and spread out his threatening letter from Sennacherib, of Assyria. The experience is recorded in Isaiah 37:14-20.

Sennacherib is taunting Hezekiah and reminding him of all the previous victories of the Assyrians. He told Hezekiah that the God of Israel would never be able to save them now, and that he shouldn't be deceived into thinking he would be saved.

Hezekiah prayed. He reminded God that everything that Sennacherib had said about his conquests was true, but he also told the Lord that because He was the God of Abraham, Isaac, and Israel, that he knew that God could do anything. Hezekiah pleaded for deliverance, for divine intervention.

God's response was to send the prophet Isaiah to Hezekiah with this message: "Thus says the God of Israel, "Because you have prayed . . . I will deliver this city and save it" (Isa.37:21, 35).

The AWA Board made the decision to move forward, and agreed to pay the $10,000 premium and to ask God to somehow provide it. Surely He hadn't brought them this far—to give up now. So they sent word to Europe that they would accept the coverage, and the premium. The insurance company's response almost knocked them down. The company said that they'd somehow miscalculated the risk involved; the annual premium would be $25,000.

The AWA group saw this impossibility as a renewed call to their knees, and as God calling them to a new level of trust. They saw no human answer. Every other company they'd contacted had been kind but firm. Now their last hope was out of reach.

"Lord," they prayed, "we believe You sent this airplane in answer to our prayers and the needs of Guyana. It is nearly ready to go, but to protect others it needs at least liability insurance. We can do nothing more. So we ask that You will supernaturally intervene in this process and provide the insurance with a revised quote." And then, in a stretch of faith, they added, "and please make it less than the original $10,000. We will give You all the glory."

From the book *Christ's Object Lessons:* "When perplexities arise, and difficulties confront you, look not for help to humanity. Trust all with God. . . . It is not the capabilities you now possess or ever will have that will give you success. It is that which the Lord can do for you. We need to have far less confidence in what man can do and far more confidence in what God can do for every believing soul" (p. 146).

A new message arrived at breakfast time the next morning. The insurance company had located an underwriter willing to cover the plane. The plane would now be covered by insurance anywhere in the United States, and in the Caribbean, but not Guyana. The new quote was faxed to AWA. The total annual premium: $500!

More prayer. More waiting for God's work to unfold. Then the European company again contacted AWA with the welcome news that Guyana was now included! At the same price—$500!

I'll tell you where there is a group of students who believe that God is still willing and able to meet the needs of His people when they step out boldly in faith to do His bidding. Their faith experience is an ongoing one, continually requiring an increasing dependence on God in the face of increasing challenges. But He is not only the author, but the finisher of our faith, and their faith grows.

As David sent out the wonderful news by e-mail to the many who had been praying for and assisting in the project, he wondered how the non-Christians who'd been interested might react. He decided that they too should know "the rest of the story."

A friend in Guyana, who had never committed his life to God, replied, "I have been faced with the absolute reality that God does hear and listen, and I will reopen dialogue with Him again."

And the Author and Finisher of our faith will be faithful to him as well.

It's one of His names.

PROMISES

Are there rewards for trusting God and putting confidence in Him? Jeremiah 17:7 tells us, "But blessed are those who trust in the Lord and have made the Lord their hope and confidence" (NLT).

Be assured that God is watching over you (Ps. 121:8).

God is in charge over the world (John 16:33).

·